12 Strategies That Will End Female Bullying

Girl Wars

Cheryl Dellasega, Ph.D., & Charisse Nixon, Ph.D.

A FIRESIDE BOOK
PUBLISHED BY
SIMON & SCHUSTER

New York

London

Toronto

Sydney

Singapore

FIRESIDE
Rockefeller Center
1230 Avenue of the Americas
New York, NY 10020

For information regarding special discounts for bulk purchases,
please contact Simon & Schuster Special Sales at 1-800-456-6798
or business@simonandschuster.com

Sample letter and response on pages 209–10 reprinted with permission from
STUDIO 2B Collection, 11-13, copyright © 2002, Girl Scouts of the United
States of America, 420 Fifth Avenue, New York, NY, 10018, www.girlscouts.org.

DESIGNED BY ELINA D. NUDELMAN

Manufactured in the United States of America

10 9 8 7 6 5 4 3 2 1

Library of Congress Cataloging-in-Publication Data is available.
ISBN 0-7432-4987-9

To the woman who made this happen, my agent, Laureen Rowland, and to the mysterious man who has been doing my laundry and fixing my meals.

—*Cheryl*

To my two precious girls, Katie and Abby, for all your trusting love and unconditional acceptance. You have been and continue to be the best teachers of all.

—*Charisse*

Contents

Girl
Wars

INTRODUCTION

Anna's thirteenth birthday is only a day away when her two best friends inform her with mock sadness that they won't be coming to her sleepover party.

"Tina asked us to go to the movies with her. That's way more fun than watching videos at your house and playing those stupid games your mom comes up with," they snicker, linking arms and walking away.

An older girl begins to make fun of newcomer Monica's scrawny build whenever they pass each other in the halls of their small rural high school. Even though fifteen-year-old Monica switches from wearing her favorite skirts and dresses to jeans, soon everyone is calling her "chicken legs" and cackling when she passes.

At ten, Lucy hates playground. Every day when the teacher is distracted, a boy will swoop up and snap the back of Lucy's new bra, which barely contains her B-cup breasts. Worse yet is the betrayal of girls, who cluster together and laugh when that happens. Even Lucy's former friends have started sticking out their chests mockingly and strutting behind her.

Day after day, fifteen-year-old Shantal and her crowd of friends face off against fourteen-year-old Erika and her group. In the cafeteria of their inner-city school, Shantal calls Erika a "slut" because she is dating Reese, a good-looking seventeen-year-old. In return, Erika shoves past Shantal and mutters "bitch" just loud enough to be heard. The confrontations grow more and more heated until one day between classes Erika punches Shantal in the face, an encounter that escalates into a brawl requiring police intervention.

What do these young women and their friends have in common? All are caught up in the whirlwind of relational aggression, wounded by the words and actions of another girl. Even Erika and Shantal, who work to maintain "tough girl" stances at all costs, are scared, hurt, and insecure underneath.

Relational aggression (RA), also called female bullying, is the use of relationships, rather than fists, to hurt another. Rumors, name calling, cliques, shunning, and a variety of other behaviors are the weapons girls use against one another on an everyday basis in schools, sports, recreational activities, and even houses of worship. The increasing incidence of physical confrontations between girls, like Erika and Shantal's are often preceded by escalating relational aggression.

Most women can recall an incident of RA in their own past, but the seriousness of these behaviors is reaching new proportions, resulting in criminal charges, school shootings, and suicides. Why are today's girls so willing to be this cruel to one another?

When psychologist Mary Pipher wrote her bestselling book *Reviving Ophelia* in the mid-1990s, she suggested we need to "work together to build a culture that is less complicated and more nurturing, less violent and sexualized, and more growth producing." If anything, the world of adolescent girls is now more complicated, violent, and sexualized as well as less nurturing than when Dr. Pipher first proposed her agenda for change.

Today's young women are subtly influenced to interact in ways that reduce rather than enhance their underlying power to connect with one another. Bombarded with messages about their physical appearance at an early age, they are expected to dress provocatively while maintaining straight "A" averages and excelling at sports. They are labeled as mean "Queen Bees" but given no alternatives for more positive behaviors. Their bodies are reaching physical maturity earlier and earlier, yet their cognitive skills remain anchored in adolescence. Role models for today's teens are not powerful women who have succeeded because of their persistence and kindness to others, but rather superstar singers acting like sexy schoolgirls and movie stars firing machine guns or using martial arts on opponents while wearing skintight jumpsuits. No wonder young women find themselves in a state of extreme confusion, unsure of how to relate to either themselves or others.

The good news is that all across the country, mothers, girls, and others are finding ways to help adolescents feel more secure about their own abilities and safe in their relationships with others. Slowly, their efforts are changing the "girl poisoning" culture Mary Pipher first lamented nearly a decade ago, transforming behavior from cruel to kind.

Do all girls have the capacity to be kind? We believe girls are *not* inherently cruel, and that although behaviors such as jealousy, gossiping, and joining cliques may be normal in terms of what we *expect*, they are not what we have to *accept*. Based on our work with hundreds of young women in both our professional and personal lives, as well as extensive research, evaluation, and input from other experts on the subject, Charisse and I know that not only can girls be kind, they feel better about themselves when they are. We call this behavior confident kindness, because the ability to be caring and supportive of others is only meaningful if it comes from an inner sense of security and self-esteem.

It is our role as adults to guide young women to form more positive self-identities, which will in turn lead to more supportive relationships with others. That's what this book is all about. How can mothers, young girls, or any other concerned party overcome RA? In this book, input from four important sources is used to identify twelve key strategies that both girls and adults can use.

First, girls who have been involved in RA share their stories, either in their own words or via interviews. These young women offer advice on how to deal with RA and share ways in which they turned their lives around—either on their own or with help from others.

A second source is the wisdom of mothers and other adults who have helped young women deal with RA. These include fathers, coaches, teachers, dance instructors, and religious education counselors. Again, the situations these adults faced with adolescent girls are shared, in their own words, along with the specific actions they took, which illustrate the strategies described.

A third source of information is experts, including Dr. Charisse Nixon and myself. Efforts are under way to develop and evaluate programs that specifically address individual, school, family, and community aspects of RA. In addition, many researchers and clinicians are actively studying and identifying key interventions that can put an end to female bullying.

Finally, several organizations that focus on improving the self-esteem of girls and helping them learn more positive ways of interacting are described. These include GENAustin, a "GirlPower" program in one high school; the Boys and Girls Clubs of America; ClubOphelia.com and its premier program, Camp Ophelia; and the Ophelia Project and one of its sister chapters in Warren, Pennsylvania.

Of course, the experiences that feel most relevant to both Charisse and myself are the ones we have had as mothers of girls who are immersed in this culture of female aggression. We have seen our daughters caught up in the tumult of RA behaviors at various ages, but in keeping with the original message of *Reviving Ophelia*, we believe change is possible. Negative messages about "mean teens," which make for great press, end up stereotyping girls and creating an expectation that such behaviors are normal. The latter is particularly damaging because it perpetuates the notion that nothing can be done, because, after all, "girls will be girls."

It is our goal to focus on the strength and resiliency of young women rather than on their deficiencies. Girls have enormous relational abilities but need guidance to build those abilities into constructive assets. In this book, we will show that girls can—and must—be taught to capitalize on the strong, resourceful, positive, and powerful side that lives inside them. Anyone—male, female, young, old, individual, or group—can use these strategies to transform the culture of female aggression to one of confident kindness.

The twelve strategies are listed step-by-step for you to follow. The first, and perhaps most important, is to inform yourself and others. Although this may sound easy enough, there are many nuances of RA that affect today's girls. The four chapters devoted to this strategy will describe special situations such as the use of computers for aggression (cyber-RA) and socioeconomic differences and similarities in RA. This content is elaborated on by vignettes by girls and parents.

Strategies 2 and 3 are preventive actions you can use to develop a girl's anti-RA skills at a young age, grow her self-esteem, and equip her with positive relationship skills. Again, the real experiences of adults and girls will be shared to illustrate these principles.

The longest section of the book deals with what to do when RA occurs (Strategies 4 through 10). We begin with relatively mild incidents and progress to serious, sustained types of harassment and aggression. These strategies will help you intervene to end the aggression and hurt all girls experience when RA occurs. Not surprisingly, girls themselves have a lot to say about what helps and what doesn't; their suggestions are summarized in Strategy 10: Give Her a Tool Kit of Options.

Strategy 11 deals with changing the larger culture through individual and community programs targeted at RA. Profiles of key organizations are provided so you can replicate similar efforts in your own home and community. Finally, you will be guided through the steps needed to develop your own action plan.

The book ends with appendices, which are by no means comprehensive but which provide further information on resources, along with a self-assessment quiz on your RA quotient. Sources for further help are also identified.

We frequently mention middle school as the context for working with girls since this is a time when gender differences emerge in RA, but in reality the strategies apply to preschool through young adulthood. While our focus is girl vs. girl aggression, we acknowledge that boys can and do engage in RA, just in different contexts and less often.

Throughout the book, we have taken the liberty of changing names and details where we feel it is appropriate. Where girls specifically requested their names be used with their stories we did so, but all participants can be contacted through Cheryl Dellasega at opheliasmother@aol.com.

In the coming years, there will be increasing pressure to create environments that help young women feel safe. Strategies such as the ones we offer are an important first step in changing the culture to make it better for both adolescent girls and ourselves.

In a farewell letter to me, one thirteen-year-old summarized her feelings after attending a week-long camp specifically for middle-school girls: "I know now that there are other ways to act. For me, this means walking away when I'm upset or politely asking for more information about why the aggressor feels the way she does. Just knowing about relational aggression will help me be a different person in the next school year." It is our hope that every girl—and adult—can learn a better way to relate to others, to be confident and kind, and to feel better about herself in the process. This book is a how-to for accomplishing these goals.

—*Cheryl Dellasega, Ph.D.*

Strategy 1:
INFORM YOURSELF AND OTHERS

THE RA FACTS OF LIFE

Yeah, that's how girls are, women too. You know, cat fights. Meow.

—ADULT WOMAN PARTICIPATING IN A
CONVERSATION ABOUT GIRLS HURTING GIRLS

What It Is

Bullying, harassing, victimizing, meanness, relational aggression: these words are all used interchangeably in reference to the behavior of girls. The term *relational aggression* (RA) was coined by researcher Nicki Crick from the University of Minnesota to describe the use of *relationships* to harm others. This behavior can be so subtle it is often missed by adults, but it can also escalate to an ongoing *RA drama* that lasts for days and even weeks. That's why, so often, RA is not a clear-cut, on-off situation but exists on a continuum of mild to extreme.

The process of using relationships to hurt another involves an aggressor (the bully or tormentor), a victim (the target), and often one or more bystanders or girls in the middle (GIM). It is not at all unusual for a girl who has been victimized to retaliate by becoming aggressive to another or for girls to play all three roles in different types of relationships. To better understand the dynamics of RA, it is important for both girls and adults to recognize the behaviors as well as the motivating factors.

Why It Happens

Ironically, *all* girls who engage in this dynamic are experiencing some underlying fear and insecurity. The aggressor may be worried about her ability to remain "on top," so she uses manipulation and control of others to avoid having her own flaws exposed. The victim often lacks the confidence to stand up for herself and may accept harassment because inside she feels it is deserved or true. Girls in the middle are also afraid and lack the self-esteem to take a stand; often they may join in the aggression either passively or overtly to avoid being targeted themselves.

Unlike males, women typically forge their identities through relationships with others. At all ages, women are more oriented toward outward connections with others. Even in sports situations, girls are social. One coach comments, "If I got a bunch of boys together who didn't know each other and sent them out to play soccer, they wouldn't think twice about it. They'd go out and play, then go off the field and never think twice about seeing each other again. Not so with girls. They need to know who is the leader, who they might become friends with, who's nice, who's popular, all of that stuff before they can play anything."

Here are some basic facts about RA, which you may feel free to reproduce. (Or check Appendix B for details on obtaining quantities of a full-size, flyer with resources and illustrations.)

Relational What?

A recent report from the Families and Work Institute asked 1,001 adolescents in the fifth through twelfth grades the following question: "If you could make one change that would help stop the violence that young people experience today, what would that change be?" Interestingly, the majority of young people talked about *emotional violence;* relational aggression is a type of emotional violence.

Relational aggression (RA) is a psychological term that signifies the use of relationships to hurt peers. Compared to other forms of aggression, such as physical violence, RA is quieter, more insidious, and harder to detect. It encompasses starting rumors, spreading gossip, teasing, creating or joining cliques, deliberately excluding another girl, and many of the stereotypical behaviors associated with girls (and women), and like most behaviors, it exists on a continuum from mild to extreme.

RA is a phenomenon that can affect boys as well, particularly in opposite-sex relationships. It appears in peer, family, and romantic contexts as well as in and out of school. Children in preschool through post-secondary have displayed behaviors that are relationally aggressive. Increasingly the computer is used to deliver negative messages.

The damage occurs because RA prevents girls from aligning with one another during an important time in their psychosocial development and instead turns them into adversaries. This way of interacting, through relationships that are a source of harassment rather than happiness, can deprive girls of a valuable support system: her peers.

Research on RA has shown that

- Relationally aggressive behavior is evident in all age groups from preschool through adulthood.

- For students in grades three through six, relational aggression is a stronger predictor of future social maladjustment than overt physical aggression.

- Girls are more likely to use RA *within* their own friendship circles, in comparison to boys, who tend to aggress *outside* their friendship circles.

- Girls who are relationally aggressive are also less likely to show empathy for others.

- Girls are more likely to approve of and use relational aggression; boys are more likely to approve of and use physical aggression.

- Relationally aggressive girls are more likely to believe that aggressive behavior is acceptable and even normal. For example, girls with high RA tendencies are also likely to believe that it is generally okay to spread rumors about someone else.

- Relational aggression is connected to peer rejection, decreased acts of prosocial behavior, and antisocial and borderline personality features in young adults.

- Relational aggression may be as strong a risk factor for future delinquency, crime, and substance abuse as physical aggression.

- Both victims and initiators of RA have a higher incidence of serious mental health problems such as depression, loneliness, alienation, emotional distress, and isolation.

- At the college level, prior experience with RA has been associated with bulimic symptoms.

- Older adolescents with a well-formed identity (young women who are goal-directed) are less likely to be relationally aggressive.

- Older adolescents with a well-developed moral identity (young women who know their values and act consistently with them) are less likely to be relationally aggressive.

- Studies show that RA is linked to physical violence.

- A recent case in Williamsport, Pennsylvania, involved a fourteen-year-old high school student who wanted desperately to be part of the "popular" crowd at her school but was routinely ridiculed and excluded. The RA drama intensified until she brought a gun to school and shot the girl she believed to be her chief tormentor. The shooter's attorney, George Lepley, said on record that the girl had been subjected to "a lot of name-calling, derogatory comments, and innuendoes." Many of the young girls I've worked with describe situations where emotional violence (RA) triggers physical confrontation. As Linda, a precocious twelve-year-old, told me, "If words don't work, after a while, I'll just pop the other girl in the mouth." According to a recent national survey, over half of young people who have been rejected or ignored have also been hit, shoved, kicked, or tripped at least once in the past month, compared to one-quarter of young people who have not been victims of RA.

- The Families and Work Institute report also highlights that adolescents want to see changes in their *culture* more than in their parents or schools. They report feeling peer and social pressure to follow and conform as a way to protect themselves. (For the full report see www.familiesandwork.org.)

Girls also need to be educated about RA. As an adult, you can provide key information. Use the words *relational aggression* or *RA*, but make sure she understands what they mean—bullying, aggression, meanness, and other hurtful behaviors. Spell out what RA is, how it hurts girls, who is usually involved, and why it happens, and assure her it can be changed. Start talking about relational aggression early on—preschool is when these behaviors begin to surface—and share stories of other girls with her so she knows she's not alone. (For the flyer "Wary Mary or Savvy Sue: Which Are You? A Primer of RA Facts for Girls," see Appendix B.)

Here are one girl's words on her experience with RA and how she dealt with it.

WORD WARS

Why are girls mean to girls? My mother told me they were jealous, my father told me they were simply mean, my oldest sister told me that's the way girls act, and my other sister just shrugged and said it happened to her too. None of this took away the pain of irreversible wounds. When boys are angry, they get physical, sometimes causing bruises or broken bones, but words are the most dangerous weapon. They sting, they last, and girls seem to have a way with words that are more vicious and attack the inner self.

She was my best friend of five years. I considered her my sister, loved her more than life itself. We promised to be friends forever and mixed our blood to seal the promise, but I drifted into honors classes as she drifted into mainstream. We made new friends and saw less and less of each other. There was not a fateful day, no final fight that I can recall.

"The most beautiful discovery that true friends can make is that they can grow separately without growing apart," or so I thought. One day I e-mailed her: "I love you." In bold letters I got back a letter declaring our friendship in the past.

Tears have never felt so hot nor pain so raw. Life changed. Her words didn't just hit a nerve; they traveled into my bloodstream and flowed throughout. My heart is what hurt the most, but the worst pain was still to come. The rumors were yet to be spread.

Another girl, who was a friend to us both, sent me the cruelest message I have ever received. Littered with four-letter words, her message told me I didn't have a right to live and said she would see to it I didn't. The threats hurt, but the most painful part said I had never been a good friend to either her or my best friend.

My parents saw the threatening mail and burst at the seams. My dad wanted to go to the police; my mom wanted to call her house. I just wanted a hug. In the end my mom called her mom, and eventually I got an apology, but it didn't mean anything. Words are not erasable. You can't say them and then delete their existence. Even if I forgive, which I have, I can't forget. To this day, I don't know what happened. I pass them in the hall, I see their smiles, and I fade away, into that oblivion that they have destined for me.

I don't know why girls hurt girls. I do know that I have been punched in the face, kicked in the leg, I have even withstood heart surgery, but nothing has been so painful as losing a best friend, a sister, my better half . . . all over words.

—Danielle Siegel, age 18, New York

WHY GIRLS ARE PRONE TO RA

*One day she couldn't get enough attention from her dad
and me, and the next day she wanted to spend every free
minute with her friends. If she's not actually with them,
she's talking to them on the phone or chatting with them
online. We practically have to make a reservation to
spend an evening with her.*
    —MOTHER OF A TWELVE-YEAR-OLD GIRL

Is there any other age as delightful or frustrating as adolescence? During this time, a glimpse of the woman-to-be emerges and gradually becomes more defined as a girl balances separation from parents with integration into peer groups and relationships.

For those of us who experienced adolescence decades ago, the teenage years can feel like foreign territory—easy to get lost in, with few recognizable road signs. Part of developing a plan to prevent and combat RA involves an appreciation for the normal but complex changes that occur in the way a girl thinks and feels during this time, many of which make her vulnerable to RA interactions.

The Geography of Adolescence

The teen years are by their very nature a time of change and transition, both physically and socially. Only infancy involves more physical and mental growth than the preteen and teen years! This maturing process has the potential to be both exciting and stressful to a girl; the more changes she has to deal with, the more stress she is likely to experience. Imagine having to adjust to the momentous move from grade to middle school while your body changes on a near-daily basis. At the same time you must try to figure out who you are as an individual and, somehow, fit in with a group you like. No wonder it may take several attempts involving dramatically different roles and identities to navigate this process, and no wonder parents have a hard time keeping up with the personas. As one mother summarized her daughter's ninth grade, "She changed on a weekly basis. First it was the punk, then the prep, then the jock, then the skater. I forget what else there was. Of course, each of these new looks required a complete change of wardrobe . . . Luckily she had a job and paid for the clothes herself."

Relationships with the opposite sex come into play during this time too. Girls have to figure out how to relate to boys. What are the rules? What is my role? Does he make the rules? What am I supposed to do? are all common dilemmas. Without positive role models or a reliable adult to consult, young women may come to accept the sexualized media images of teens as their norm.

How Thinking and Social Relationships Change

Girls at this age are naturally egocentric. To their preoccupied way of thinking, everyone else is observing and reacting to them, which means that even the slightest social gaffe on their part will take on enormous significance.

Another characteristic of adolescence is uniqueness. Each girl views herself as different, contending that no one else could possibly understand how she feels. She will sincerely believe she is the only girl in her whole school who worries about not having the right friends, enough friends, or one true friend.

Although an adolescent's mind is becoming more flexible and able to think about the perspective of others, adolescents experience negative emotions more intensely than adults. What seem like relatively trivial events to grown-ups can have a dramatic impact on girls.

While the exact timetable can differ from child to child, social development tends to follow this pattern:

In middle childhood (ages six to ten) children recognize that people have feelings but focus on more observable details, like what people are wearing, what they look like, and how they behave. At this age a girl judges things good or bad according to their consequences, not according to the motivations behind them. It is hard for her to understand that someone aggresses against her because of insecurity; she only knows that her feelings are hurt.

In the later elementary school years (ages nine to eleven), girls are trying their best to please others and be seen as a "good person." They care about others, but this can be a double-edged sword: they care tremendously what others think! Programmed by culture to place the esteem of others first, a girl can be so desperate for the approval of others she enters relationships where she is manipulated and controlled by others. Fear of rejection becomes overwhelming; "popularity" is the ultimate goal.

During early adolescence (ages eleven to fourteen), close friendships gain even more importance and girls pay less attention to parents. Increasingly, they are concerned with acceptance from same-sex peers and will conform to group norms for dress, music, and hobbies, a behavior that peaks in middle school. Even though they may not always show it, girls at this age still see parents as a major resource for both information and emotional support.

Middle adolescence (fifteen to seventeen) is marked by even stronger ties to a peer group, as this is the time when independence and development of identity are critical. At this stage a girl will start to think about academic, social, and vocational goals for herself, which is all part of the identity formation process. Her willingness to share and cooperate increases as she sees herself as part of a community. A teen's peer group as well as family network will serve as sources for advice and will strongly influence her lifestyle, ideas, and beliefs.

By late adolescence (seventeen to nineteen), a sense of independence is normal as girls begin to show greater self-reliance and more concern for others. Peers are viewed more as a resource where opinions can be sought and considered rather than dictated.

At each stage peers make a valuable contribution to a girl's development because they provide a training ground for relationship skills, skills that often spill over into a romantic context. For example, if a girl learns to manipulate and hurt others in same-sex friendships, she is more likely to use these same behaviors with a boyfriend. On the other hand, a girl who is repeatedly victimized by others may come to accept this treatment as normal and stay in unhealthy relationships.

Underlying all relationships is the issue of trust. In adolescence, girls learn whom to trust and whom not to. They are beginning to navigate the waters of intimate relationships and finding out firsthand how trust is established and lost. This trial-and-error process can often be very painful, especially for girls, who are oriented toward using intimacy with others to discover who they are.

Empathy

These years are an ideal time to provide guidance to girls because they are at a point cognitively where they can think about the perspective of others. This insight can contribute to either constructive (empathetic) or destructive (hurtful) behavior patterns. Girls who feel secure are more likely to adopt the former, while those who feel threatened will rely on the latter.

Charisse's research shows that girls who are relationally aggressive are more likely to be less empathetic. The logical question is then, Can we teach empathy? The answer is, Absolutely!

Empathy involves three steps:

1. Being able to identify another's feelings. "Maybe she copies the way I dress because she wants to be like me," or "Sara looks like she is feeling sad."

2. Taking another's perspective. "If I were new to the school, I'd want someone to ask me to eat lunch with her."

3. Showing empathetic behavior, such as putting your hand on someone's shoulder, going to stand next to her, sending a friendly card or note.

A Word About Physical Changes

In addition to their social and cognitive development, girls are changing physically as well. Dr. Angela Huebner, family and child development specialist at Virginia Tech University, identifies the following physical changes as primary.

- Rapid gains in height and weight. During a one-year growth spurt, girls can gain an average of 3.5 inches in height. This spurt, which typically occurs two years earlier for girls than for boys, may make them appear older than they really are.

- Development of secondary sex characteristics. During puberty, changing hormonal levels play a role in activating the development of secondary sex characteristics. Teens may be concerned because they are more developed than their peers (early maturers) or less developed (late maturers). Being out of developmental step with peers is a concern to adolescents because most just want to fit in.

- Continued brain development. Recent research suggests that the connections between neurons affecting emotional, physical, and mental abilities are incomplete until late adolescence. This could explain why some teens seem to be inconsistent in controlling their emotions, impulses, and judgments.

Dr. Huebner's article on this topic, which includes actions for parents, can be located at http://www.ext.vt.edu/pubs/family/350-850/350-850.html. It's worth a read! Two other excellent resources include the books *Too Old for That, Too Young for This: Your Survival Guide to Middle School* (Free Spirit Press, 2000) by Harriet Mosatche, Ph.D., and Karen Unger of the Girl Scouts of America (for girls and boys) and *Raising Good Children* (Bantam Books, 1994) by Dr. Thomas Lickona.

Mothers and Daughters

Often the best and worst aspects of moms and girls get accentuated during adolescence, when a daughter needs to decide how she wants to be both like and different from her mother. Mothers may experience this dynamic as rejection and ask, Why does my daughter seem to reject me and all the values I've tried to instill in her? According to input from hundreds of girls, the grounding received from parents is an important touchstone in their lives and provides a reference point for major decisions they make, whether moms and dads realize it or not. We can't stress enough that caring adults who provide unconditional love and support are critical for healthy development, even if every message you get from her seems to suggest the opposite!

Cultural Influences

While we all have an inherent need for connectedness and mutual dependency, increasingly our culture promotes competition and independence. At a time when girls are striving with all their energy to make friends and be part of a group, they are often given subtle and not so subtle messages that encourage them to focus on individual achievement at all costs.

In addition, our current culture celebrates sameness and a hierarchical order of social relationships, a preference often manifested in what we know as cliques. At a recent workshop, one mom commented: " . . . at least my daughter is part of the 'right' clique. She should be protected from some of this." As adults, we need to be aware of what cliques are teaching our daughters and to question whether those exclusive groupings teach and reinforce the fundamental principles of prejudice and discrimination. Beware of the "right" clique!

Conformity to peers peaks in middle school, when there is pressure for a girl to act and dress like others, whether or not she agrees with their behavior, sense of style, and values. The following story shows how trying to gain friends by pleasing others can backfire.

SEAT 21

Most of this story takes place in seat 21, my assigned bus seat. Even if the popular kids who sat in the back with me didn't talk to me (or if they did and made me feel like I was two inches big), it didn't matter. I would still sit there. Whenever one of the popular girls took my seat (21), I felt lucky and proud that she had chosen it out of any on the bus. Until Nan.

Nan lived about two blocks away from me, one of three kids in my neighborhood who were my age. Of course I wanted to be her friend. She had long blond hair and blue eyes and was a little taller than me. She was beautiful compared to me, or that's at least what I thought at the time.

She and one of her older sisters became cheerleaders and were really good at it. She convinced me to try out, but they really shouldn't have tried to stuff a chubby little girl into an extra-small miniskirt and midriff. When I didn't make the squad, there were no words spoken but the friendship was over. We began to hang around with different groups of people and slowly became enemies.

Cheerleaders versus the Freaks. My group didn't really care what they called us, but we called ourselves Freaks, and we were proud to be Freaks. To us, the worst thing was to be what they were: a bunch of "preppies." Don't get me wrong. Deep, deep, deep down inside I might have still wanted to be one of them. After all, I still sat in seat 21.

The taunting became worse as seventh grade went on, and one day Nan turned to me and said, "Sabrina, I don't like your curly hair. I'm going to beat you up someday at the bus stop." For a seventh grader that comment could be heartbreaking, but I just tucked it away and asked her, "When?" She was too scared ever to fight me and it never did happen.

Now that I look back at it, it all sounds really stupid. But the experience literally changed my life. It made me the freak I am today.

—Sabrina Messina, Pennsylvania

As a girl changes and matures, so do relationships with peers. What remains constant is the importance of her social life, which often becomes all-important, even shaping her into the woman she will be. The fluidness of the aggressor/victim roles are highlighted by the next story, as is the changing importance of a girl's social landscape.

**Girl
Wars**

When I was in the primary school, I was president of student council and had four good friends. Although we didn't realize it then, the jealousy, betrayal, and pain were just beginning. As third and fourth graders, the four of us walked around in matching jackets, like the Pink Ladies of *Grease*. We were envied by girls and crushed on by guys.

I was the first to have a "boyfriend," if you could call him that. We wrote each other notes and gave hugs good-bye. It was the cool thing to do, so the other girls of the group decided to have boyfriends too. We were too young at this age, but it made us feel good about ourselves; it gave us a sense of belonging.

In fourth grade we had a sleepover at our school. My boyfriend and I were the only ones to slow dance. All the other kids looked on as I was in my own dream world. Of course my throne of ice was melted when we broke up a month later, to the delight of my best friends.

I got my period early in middle school and decided to tell a girl whom I considered a best friend. She told my boyfriend and my other best friends. I felt violated. My hurt led to anger and I began to distrust my "friends." Since I couldn't find loyalty in girls, I looked to petty middle school relationships with guys. We didn't go anywhere, but we would eat together at lunch and call each other on the phone. Finally, my older sister pointed out how I was using guys. I also began to look at my friends and how we treated each other. I knew some things had to change.

During hockey season of my seventh-grade year I began to play well. My same group of friends also played. I was scoring goals, and although you'd think they would be happy for me, they weren't. They would do anything for a goal not to be mine. It really angered me, but I tried to ignore it.

When I ran for president of the middle school in the eighth grade, I was crushed by a friend whom I believed to be different from the rest. When I handed out campaign stickers, two sixth graders came up to me and asked if they could have new ones because a blond-headed girl had ripped them off. They told me her name, and it was my best friend. Although I won, I cried and cried that night, feeling like I didn't have any true friends in the world.

After that day I threw myself into activities: I maintained a 4.0 GPA and was determined to depend on myself. I talked to my aunt, who was the girl that everyone wanted to be like in her high school days. She told me girls were rude to her too and it's just a part of life. It meant a lot to me knowing that even she, who seemed perfect, had to deal with jealous girls.

When high school rolled around, I was confident with my new self. I was happy and I'm sure it made some girls very envious. Hockey season went the same as usual with girls yelling their usual comments, but I prevailed. I ran for class president and lost. I wasn't used to this and I had to deal with it. My parents were understanding and helped me see that life isn't always about getting what you want. It is also about getting hurt.

Now when one of my friends hurts me, I laugh inside. I see her insecurities and realize it's nothing I can change. I can't make everyone happy, but most importantly I need to be true to myself and find real happiness within.

—Meghan N., ninth grade, Pennsylvania

Any mother of a teenage girl will nod her head at the way Meghan's story underscores both the importance of friends and the changes in relationships that take place over the school years. Superimpose the social challenge of finding and keeping friends on top of a body that literally changes from day to day and you have adolescence, one of the most exciting—and potentially dangerous—stages of a girl's life.

UNDERSTANDING CYBER-RA

She's the Queen of Mean online.

—A TEENAGE GIRL DISCUSSING ANOTHER GIRL'S
OUT OF SCHOOL BEHAVIOR

Computers have offered girls yet another venue to communicate with one another and have allowed them to expand their relationships to global proportions. E-mails, instant messages (IMs), and chat rooms are now channels through which hurtful interactions can and do occur. Any method of communication that allows for anonymous interaction will change the level of responsibility and accountability a girl feels for her behavior. The ability to conceal one's identity frees aggressors to be crueler and makes victims even more fearful because they don't know who their enemies are.

Recently the Girl Scouts of America gathered information about the Internet habits of over a thousand girls age thirteen to eighteen. According to these teens, the pluses of Internet communication include the ability to locate a variety of information quickly and easily and the opportunity for an outlet to express emotions that might otherwise not get shared. Being proficient in the use of the computer and Internet also gives girls status with their friends. The negative aspects of computer use are that 58 percent of girls are more computer savvy than their parents, and many admitted that they broke their parents' rules for computer use. In personal interviews many girls confessed to sending "evil e-mails" to friends when angry and using meaner behavior online than they would in person. (For a full version of this interesting study, *The Net Effect*, go to www.girlscouts.org.)

Cyber-RA Hurts As Much As Face-to-Face RA

Despite the fact that girls cannot see one another, the messages they receive via computer can be as damaging—if not more so—than those received in live interactions. Anonymous aggression can leave a girl feeling even more vulnerable and scared than having to face her tormentors.

One young woman shared a story of being devastated when several youths she didn't even know flamed her by mass mailing hurtful messages to her while she was in a chat room. Another girl had changed screen name five times in as many months to avoid being stalked by her peers. Still others tell stories of being aggressed against by either friends or strangers through the computer.

A police officer stationed at a large suburban high school recounts how she regularly deals with the effects of cyber-RA: "Check out the website www.xanga.com. It's a huge problem because it's free, and girls use it to create their own web pages. Many girls use these as a site for an online diary, and then there is a spot for others to comment on your site, thoughts, etc. As you can imagine, last year several girls used it to trash other girls. The initial RA occurred outside of school, but it continued the next day with looks, comments, sometimes nearly to the point of physical confrontation. I say it's a problem because we as police can't do anything—the girl doesn't actually *send* a harassing message to another girl, she merely *posts* something negative on her own site—but I've had girls tell me this type of RA has made them so depressed they've considered suicide.

"When girls get brought in to see me because of harassment that started online, they're amazed to hear it's a crime. I tell them, 'If you were eighteen, I'd be charging you with a crime right now.' They don't believe it's as damaging as it is."

The following story tells how one girl discovered via the Internet who her friends really were and stresses the need for adult supervision in an activity that encourages faceless aggression.

ON AGAIN/OFF AGAIN

Ann was my best friend at the beginning of the year. We had the same classes and walked together all the time. One day I noticed she was ignoring me, so I asked her if something was wrong. She just shook her head but kept ignoring me. Finally I asked her why she was mad. I couldn't remember doing anything mean to her, so I was really confused.

She told me someone had told her I was saying mean things behind her back. She wouldn't tell me who it was, but obviously it was someone convincing. Although I hadn't done anything wrong, I apologized because she meant a lot to me. I didn't have very many friends, and I couldn't afford to lose her.

We were best friends again until a month later, when it happened again. Now I knew she was mad at me, but again, I had done nothing wrong. I tried to stay strong and not apologize, but I just couldn't. So again I apologized, and we went back to being best friends.

On the last day of school, she totally ignored me again! Some of my other friends got the inside scoop and told me what was going on with her: she was badmouthing me. During the summer I was kind of doing my own thing and not talking to her until she started talking to me on the Internet. She was being nice, but I could feel something wasn't right. I went along with it because I'm not the kind of person who stays mad. We were still talking a little bit until she sent a message to her whole buddy list saying not to talk to me because I am a disgrace to this earth. That got me really fired up, so I confronted her.

She is a bad liar. First she tried telling me that she got it off an e-mail and just *had* to send it on. Then she denied even telling me that and changed the story completely. By that point I hated her.

Luckily I had friends who told me to forget about her and that what she was saying wasn't true. In a situation like this, it is best to find out who your real friends are and stick with them.

—Hilary, a teen

Another mother shares an incident involving serious threats and harassment, confirming that a continuum of RA behaviors can exist even online.

WHO?

Today, there are so many avenues of communication, it's hard to know who, when, where, and why. We not only have our real names, but also screen names, so even the who is a mystery. Who is talking to our children? Who is harassing my daughter?

During spring break my teenage daughter was on the computer talking to her friends through instant messaging. She received an IM from an individual pretending to be a friend. They started playing the guessing game, "Who is it?"

I had to run out on an errand when my daughter asked me to stay and told me she was scared. The sender of the IM had turned mean and angry toward my daughter. This person was no friend—or was she or he? Our only clue was the screen name, which I concluded belonged to an adult, probably a mother.

At this point even I became scared. Someone was scaring my daughter by telling her, "I know where you live," "I'm watching you right now," "I know that you dance," and other personal details. He/she went on to say, "I'm going to get you," and "You better watch over your shoulder."

I printed out the conversation and made my daughter sign off. I went on with my screen name to e-mail the person who had threatened my daughter, only to discover the screen name had already been deleted. I had no way of tracing him or her.

My daughter was afraid to leave the house. She panicked every time I needed to go anywhere. The situation victimized our whole family.

After reading the printout of the conversation over and over, I picked up more clues. This person mentioned my daughter's dance classes more than once, so I went to the teachers at the dance school. In the beginning of the year my daughter had provided information that was distributed to all the dancers in each company. There were older girls in the dance company, and I concluded it was one of them.

The dance company director made an announcement that let everyone know the consequences if a dancer was held responsible for the e-mail to my daughter. As we were leaving the school the next night, a man approached me, introducing himself as "Beth's" dad. Beth was sixteen, a good dancer, and one of my daughter's role models. She had always been nice and joked around with my daughter a lot. I didn't want to believe it was her.

Her dad said he had the information I wanted. Beth and her fourteen-year-old brother came over and admitted they had used their mom's screen name to scare my daughter.

The mom was crying and pleading with me not to tell. She apologized over and over. This was a girl I liked, and I didn't want to see her dancing career shattered. I respected her parents' honesty and integrity in coming forward. They offered to have their children do chores for me, but all I ever wanted to know was who, when, where, and why my daughter was harassed.

Who: Beth and her brother. When: During spring break. Where: Their house. Why: They were bored.

—Sim Suleki, Florida

Cyber Skills for Preventing RA

Detective Steven Beard, an eleven-year veteran of the Derry Township Police Force (Hershey, Pennsylvania) and a certified trainer in Internet safety, counsels adults and children on how to avoid these types of interactions. He offers parents these tips:

- Learn the technology. Many parents are intimidated or overwhelmed by computers, but the best way to protect your daughter is to have savvy skills yourself.

- Know where she is. Just as you would ask where your daughter is going on a night out with friends, you should know what she is doing on the computer. There are even software programs available for this purpose, or the simple command "ctrl-I" while on Internet Explorer will give a history of where your girl has been online. America Online has a special drop-down menu next to the URL line (where you type in web addresses) for this same purpose.

- Don't give any child control of master passwords.

- Any behavior that is a crime in real life is a crime on the computer. If your girl is being threatened online, you should definitely contact the police. It's important to do so within forty-eight hours so they can retrieve evidence. Simply turn off the computer and call if you don't know how to save the damaging communication.

- Check out online resources for web safety, such as www.missingkids.com (go to "Resources" and "Internet"), www.safekids.com, and www.cyberangels.org, which offers online and offline courses.

He offers the following advice for girls:

- Protect your personal information. Never give out your real name, address, phone number, or anything else that will reveal your identity and therefore make you vulnerable.

- Don't create a screen name that tells others anything personal

31

about you, and don't assume you know anything about anyone else from his or her screen name.

- Beware of identity theft. Someone can alter your screen name, or anyone else's, simply by adding an underscore or a single capital letter. Make sure you know who you're talking to—and who's talking to you.

- Be careful what you say in e-mails, chat rooms, or instant messages. Remember that others won't know your intent; they may think you're angry when you're not. It's easy to misinterpret when you can't see someone's face or hear his or her voice.

- Adopt an IRL principle: In Real Life. Your actions on the Internet should be the same as in real life.

Detective Beard suggests that parents sign a contract with their daughters that governs use of the computer and Internet. The Girl Scouts offers a downloadable version of "My Online Safety Pledge" for this purpose (http://jfg.girlscouts.org).

Other Types of Techno-RA

The computer is not the only way in which girls can indirectly aggress against one another. "Three ways" or calling one girl on the phone and getting her to talk about another girl who is actually listening in on the conversation is another common use of technology to deliver hurtful behavior. Again, monitoring her use of the telephone can help promote awareness and possibly prevent hurtful dynamics from developing. Tracing calls and using an answering machine to record conversations when harassment occurs are options for intervening.

Cyber-Alternatives

There are many creative and interesting activities for girls to pursue on the web. During a cyber-RA workshop such as e-smART: Safe Places for Cyber-Girls (see Appendix B), digital art and websites that promote positive interactions are introduced to middle school girls. Using software for image manipulation, creation of clip art and graphics, and text editing, girls can not only learn skills that may benefit them later, but avoid the boredom that provides fertile ground for RA.

WHAT IS EQUAL OPPORTUNITY RA?

Then I heard my daughter's friend say, "Hey, b——, how you doin'?" and I marched over and said, "How can you be so disrespectful to call someone you care about a name like that?"

—AFRICAN AMERICAN MOTHER OF
A FIFTEEN-YEAR-OLD GIRL

Young women today find themselves in a world that does not discriminate when it comes to RA. Virtually every girl from every type of background has been involved in some scenario involving aggression, whether on the television screen, as part of a crowd, or face-to-face.

Our Culture of Aggression

We have become desensitized to the violence girls are exposed to on a daily basis. Song lyrics and music videos give covert messages about the acceptability of aggression against women while newspapers regularly carry stories of overt crimes. Forms of aggression against young women that would be unacceptable in real life are portrayed on the television screen every day after school.

As Nathaniel Gadsden, minister, educator, and father of two teenage daughters, observes, "We adults have to be very tuned in to the fact that our society has always emphasized the outside features of girls. We say that's not true, but most young ladies grow up with a feeling of 'Am I pretty?' We have to be careful how we package things to females and be absolutely aware of the fact that in urban areas especially, lots of our young ladies are more aggressive because of the hip-hop culture and bombardment of messages about being tough. It used to be competitive aspects were not emphasized for young women, but now we're in a totally different world where they are actually encouraged to be aggressive. In videos and movies, women are shown as tough and able to fight. I work with third graders who have already learned to fight, be disrespectful, fight back, and they can't even explain why."

A family therapist who works with adolescent girls says, "Look at these issues in the context of the world in which we live, and they're not so surprising. We have a level of tolerance for violence that we didn't have in the past, which doesn't set a real good example for girls."

All too often girls are subtly encouraged to compete with and dislike one another through messages in magazine articles and television shows. An issue of a popular weekly magazine featured side-by-side profiles of Prince William and his new flatmate, an attractive model and student. The "college major" listed for him was: "Art history—and making girls swoon," while hers was "Art history—and making girls jealous."

Another advertisement illustrating this point is one for a spray-on product designed to lighten hair. The ad, which has been discontinued, featured a teenage girl in a bikini surrounded by boys as other girls looked on. The caption read, "Stop hating her and start being her."

The media message to girls is well summarized in the following piece by a young woman who created her own e-zine, www.faerytale.org/femmefatale.

CONTESTANTS

Upon turning eleven, I entreated my mother to purchase a subscription to *Fashion Magazine X*, believing that it would be a superb initiation into the sophisticated teenage world of which I was soon to become a member. I anxiously awaited its arrival in my mailbox each month, at which time I would assiduously labor at attempting to collect the pearls of wisdom encrypted in its pages. Eventually I had a proverbial necklace of knowledge, all acquired from the magazine. Among the pearls on the strand were articles like "How to Get Noticed at a Party" and "How to Get His Attention: 10 Great Beauty Tips That Really Work!" with the occasional "All About the Rivalry Between Generic Female Pop Star Y and Generic Female Pop Star Z" thrown in for variety. Whether their content comprised beauty tips relating to standing out or instructions on how to "walk sexy and get seen first," there was one key teenage girl concept I acquired an understanding of from reading the articles. This key concept was that, regardless of what else I would ever be occupied with, I would always inexorably be a contestant in a perpetual beauty contest, vying for the approval and attention of a male judge. As I understood it, this facet of female existence was inescapable, as it was the greatest determinant of one's worth. It therefore became necessary to do all I could, utilizing makeup, diet tips, and anything else which would aid my place as number one in the lifelong contest. I soon stumbled upon another invaluable piece of knowledge: if the postulate that life was a perpetual beauty contest was true, then it logically held true that every girl, everywhere, was my competitor. Every female I met was a prospective thief of my sash bearing the number one. This idea carried great significance, because it meant that I could never have a truly profound relationship with any girl, no matter how lovely she, her slip dresses, or her makeup were. For regardless of how brightly they smile at one another or how frequently they embrace, everyone knows that the contestants are all secretly plotting to procure the coveted tiara.

—Mariam Firunts, age 15, California

What would happen if girls could create their own culture? Beliefs predict behavior, so we must make an effort to change girls' expectations of what can and should be considered normal. Providing girls with an outlet to challenge their peers and adults to change the culture can be a powerful first step in actually making that change happen, as voiced in the following essay.

DIFFERENT

When black girls hurt black girls with words, they are striking out at the dark face that haunts their mirror, the specter that terrorizes them day in and day out.

Ugly. You ain't got no alibi. You ugly. I said. You ugly.

To be black and female in America is to be painfully invisible and undeniably exploited. And so the black girl suffers her blackness; she suffers her femininity. She sees other black girls as viable victims when she seeks to cast out her pain, because she has been conditioned to believe that black girls are worthless and negligible. When black girls hurt black girls with words, they are demonstrating what years of internalized racism have done to the most vulnerable members of a minority group.

She ain't cute. She ain't nothing. She black as tar. Her nose big. Her hair nappy.

In Cleveland, just a few years back, a girl stabbed another girl to death on her front lawn for taunting her about her "nappy" hair. Both girls were thirteen or fourteen years old, obviously inculcated with the mythology of "good hair" that is sadly pervasive in black culture. The finer the texture of hair, too many blacks believe, the more attractive its owner. The outraged "killer" was probably pushed over some psychological edge by her classmate's teasing. Perhaps she thought that killing the girl would destroy the idea that she was not beautiful and never would be. Who knows what she was thinking when she strode down the street with a knife in her hand?

I can't stand her. She think she cute. Forget her. She ain't nobody.

When black girls hurt black girls with words, we must do more than shake our heads and label it a shame. In Toni Morrison's *The Bluest Eye*, the author shows us, through stunning prose, how the destruction of one little black girl is really a reflection of a larger, insidious decaying of society.

Black women and men need to examine the ways in which they are complicit in helping to make their daughters victims by perpetuating the self-hatred bred by slavery, economic and class divisions within the black community, and the mindless internalization of white conceptions of black history and culture.

We all need to know that when black girls hurt black girls, they inflict wounds that leave scars, and understand that the hurts of the individual resonate powerfully in her world, spreading her pain.

—Michelle R. Smith, Ohio

Although same-sex aggression was present in biblical times (remember the story of Hagar and Sarah?) and is a constant for women, there are many variations in the ways aggression is expressed. The study of relationships between girls is still evolving, so there are no data to support that RA behaviors are different for particular ethnic groups, in urban versus rural locations, or among different economic strata. However, some people's experiences suggest that the underlying motivations and roles are consistent but the degree of aggression varies.

Poverty and Aggression

Lisa Blanton, one of the adult facilitators of Camp Ophelia and an expert in adolescent health, notes that for poor girls, an additional layer of complexity is added on to the aggression dynamic. Recalling her own experiences, she describes the effect of poverty on adolescent girls: "When she's in her home neighborhood, a girl might not feel 'less than' wearing the same outfit several times (and, believe me, clothing is a prized commodity poor girls will go to great lengths to obtain). However, when she leaves the neighborhood, the same girl will only wear that outfit periodically so as to avoid being ridiculed and made fun of by other girls. Poor girls often come from a family situation that is fractured and atypical, which only places even greater emphasis on the girl herself: her appearance and her external abilities."

Another area of sensitivity for poor black girls is hair, notes Lisa, who is African American. This is one more aspect of a girl's looks that can be targeted because if she lacks money or a caring female, she may be unable to groom her hair in a way that is socially acceptable.

In these situations girls may be even more sensitive to the comments of would-be aggressors and may respond with anger rather than passivity, because when you are poor, any criticism of who you are goes right to the heart of the things most valued and creates a powder-keg situation. Girls escalate into physical forms of violence when threatened in any way.

Solutions? Lisa Blanton feels strongly about school uniforms; she suggests that if all girls dressed the same way, some of the pressure and tension over appearances would be removed.

Pat Gadsden, co-director of Camp Ophelia, sees that the essential problem for young women of color is the same as that for all youth who are troubled—a failure to connect in ways that use their innate power. She agrees that if young women come from a poor neighborhood where aggression is the norm, they must struggle to escape yet another context that encourages hurtful behavior. "They may only be able to do this mentally in their minds," she admits, in cases where girls are surrounded by negative influences. "But hopefully there can be someone in that girl's life who can teach her to strive for better."

Pat, the mom of two teenage girls, a Girl Scout leader, and a facilitator of many youth groups, sees parallels between girls who are aggressive and girls who are leaders. "Both have tremendous leadership skills," she says. "But in the case of the aggressive girl, she is using hers to influence others in negative ways or through intimidation. If she can just learn to turn the behavior around, she could be a very positive influence."

Pat's husband, Nathaniel Gadsden, works on relationship skills with adolescents in urban schools, where he sees extreme examples of the types of aggression Lisa Blanton refers to.

He recently conducted a classroom workshop with sixth and seventh graders in which one young Hispanic girl, who was very attractive, listed her hair and her looks as her strengths.

After the project, the Reverend Gadsden saw the same young lady in the hallway, face-to-face with an African American girl, locked in an interaction that escalated to such aggression that both he and a security guard intervened. The guard told him that the young Hispanic girl, who was dating a nineteen-year-old boy, spends her days at school creating the kind of dramas they had just witnessed.

"Nowadays," Nate says, "young ladies are trying to act like boys, even act more masculine than the boys themselves do. They say degrading things to each other and try to act tough. Yet underneath that façade, there is a scared young person, no matter what they tell you. Young ladies do not feel safe underneath. Sitting in the schools, listening to teachers or administrators talk to them talk about fighting, I can see kids are afraid of other kids, especially when there are groups. Now young ladies are doing the same thing as boys used to, which is that they will fight to save face.

"More and more, suburban kids are tuned in to the same information as the urban kids and are getting the same nonsense in their heads. The most dangerous sector is wannabes—wanna be famous, tough, none of which they are. Girls or boys, they end up getting into trouble because they are easily led and follow people who will take them to jail. Suburban girls are more likely to come from a system where there are supports, so when there are problems, it causes a ripple effect and hurts so many other people. In urban areas, there aren't as many connections, so there isn't that same ripple effect."

The role of adults, he believes, is to get young women to talk about feelings, even when they say they don't care. He uses thought-provoking stories to try to get the kids talking. "I think about Jesus and how he used the parables to teach, so I do the same. I give kids a hypothetical, tell them stories, all true stuff, and then ask what they think. I have a lot of stories, so they call me the Story Man. But my goal for girls or youth is to encourage thinking skills, the same process I teach in my abstinence camp, which is to stop, think, act, and then review."

The administrator of a large social service agency recalls meeting recently with a juvenile court judge who told him that more and more urban girls are appearing in court on charges of physical aggression. The judge commented, "Two boys come in and by the time they leave, they're friends again. With the girls, the trials last half a day or more, because the girls bring all their friends and go on and on about the incident."

Another mental health worker, who runs a program that involves almost equal numbers of white, African American, and Latina girls, says she hasn't noticed any ethnic differences in the way RA is expressed. Socioeconomic status (SES) does seem to play a role, though, with poorer girls feeling a baseline insecurity not felt by those who are better off. When a girl is more aggressive, this caseworker notes the cause seems to be her particular situation (such as a family where violence is the norm) rather than her ethnicity.

A middle school counselor who works with schools that have a mixed student body in terms of both ethnicity and SES says, "I do think some of it is behavior learned from moms. In one school district I work with in particular, a very 'have' community, I see 'Queen Bee' behaviors in the moms. As I've gotten into schools with lower socioeconomic status, cultural differences emerge. Sort of like white upper-class girls face the tyranny of nice, they have to be polite and sweet, so they're less direct about assertiveness. Hispanic and black girls seem much more direct in the way they express their feelings. There needs to be a happy medium between the two groups."

While it seems clear that the additional pressure of poverty may predispose girls to overt violence, and that certain aspects of ethnicity such as hair and skin tone may be one more aspect of appearance that can be ridiculed, the solutions remain the same. Girls need to feel an inner confidence in themselves and believe in their abilities. Whether they learn these qualities from mentors and adults from backgrounds similar to or different from theirs is an interesting debate.

When recruiting counselors for Camp Ophelia, our goal was to match the ethnicity of the campers as closely as possible, but as the week wore on, it seemed the girls bonded with their mentors more on the basis of personality than skin color. Miranda Oropeza, a college freshman and volunteer at GENAustin, a nonprofit organization for adolescent girls in Texas, recalls a similar debate that took place when plans were being made to select high school mentors for the afterschool program she helped develop for middle school girls. "As someone from a diverse background myself, I was really opposed to putting girls in categories based on ethnicity. It sort of defeats the whole idea of programs to help girls get along with everyone else if you only put them with someone exactly like themselves, doesn't it? Anyway, how realistic is that? When you go out in life, you can't always be with people who are just like you," she points out.

Global RA

RA is not unique to the United States. Girls and adults from the United Kingdom, Australia, India, Canada, Greece, and New Zealand have contacted me with stories of aggression. One of them follows.

TART

Last year I decided to go to school instead of being home-schooled because I wanted to meet some friends. The good things about school were that I had friends, I liked the food, I liked the lessons, and I enjoyed going to camp. The bad thing about school was that girls started to bully me and the teachers did not listen.

I was punched two times, slapped four times, and called names. Girls started to threaten me. Then I started getting abusive phone calls.

At this point my parents went to the school to talk to the teachers, but they said there was nothing they could do. My parents then reported the harassment to the police, who traced the calls. After this, however, we never heard from the police again. This was over a year ago—I have never been back to school since.

Bullying is nasty because it hurts your feelings. If you're being bullied, you feel scared every time you go out and you get scared when you see the people that are bullying you. It made me feel upset, angry, depressed, and nervous. I was angry because the teachers didn't believe my story. I was nervous going outside in case I bumped into the girls that bullied me. I was also angry that I couldn't go back to school because I was too scared and I was upset because I missed my friends.

I think girls bully other girls because they are jealous. They bullied me because they were jealous of me going out with a boy that they fancied. I think also they didn't like the fact that I wouldn't dump him like they had demanded.

—R.A., age 13, United Kingdom

Strategies 2 and 3:
PREVENT RA
BUILD HER ANTI-RA SKILLS
AT A YOUNG AGE

You can't wait until she's an adolescent. It has to start much earlier, or else you'll be dealing with both teenage issues and relationship issues at the same time.
—FAMILY THERAPIST, ON HOW TO HELP GIRLS

While relational aggression seems to peak in the early teen years, the groundwork for such behaviors is laid long before a girl crosses the threshold of middle school. Whether as victim, aggressor, or bystander, a young woman first learns how to relate to her peers as a toddler, beginning a social education that continues throughout her life. Behaviors that get rewarded are repeated, and those that do not are abandoned. As adults, there are everyday strategies we can use to help girls enter adolescence aware and prepared, rather than clueless and scared.

She's Never Too Young
Early on, girls need to receive a strong and consistent message that any behavior that hurts another is never okay. Be specific about what behavior is acceptable and what is not. Use role-playing to act out exactly the type of interactions you hope to reward or discourage. Brainstorm with girls what to do when other girls are "mean." Although many mothers report need-

ing programs for elementary schools, the following letter suggests that even preschoolers may be an appropriate audience for "lessons in kindness":

> From my perspective, younger kids need to be reached before they set up habits and group dynamics for being mean. I have girls in first and second grade and see girls in those age groups starting down the road to meanness already. It became so difficult for my ten-year-old to cope this year that after much thought and discussion with a counselor and our pediatrician, we have put her on a mild antidepressant—a situation that saddens and infuriates me, since she is the good kid! Her self-esteem and coping skills had become so compromised, she felt there was no hope or any way out. She was lonesome and her grades dropped. The prospect of middle school seems terrifying for me unless things get better. If I have to home school her I will, but it seems that many kids will be in her same position yet without a parent who can step in like I do. What will their self-esteem be like?

The "Early" and "Late" Bloomer

The age of the onset of puberty has dropped so dramatically that it is not unusual to see fifth and sixth graders with the kind of figures that formerly belonged to much older girls. At the same time, other girls on a more leisurely timetable for development may feel inadequate next to their more mature peers.

While there is nothing an adult can do to change the physiology of a girl, it does pay to be sensitive to these issues and to be aware that girls who "blossom" early are often targets for aggression. It's a mistake to assume that a twelve-year-old girl who has the body of a sixteen-year-old will also have the emotional and cognitive skills to process and cope with hurtful comments from her peers. Even if she gets her period at age nine or ten, she remains a little girl in many ways.

Girls who are "late bloomers" may be pushed into the role of victim or aggressor by their lack of physical attributes. Feeling insecure about one's body can drive a young woman to aggress against another, while the emphasis society places on appearance may lead victims to believe that they truly are inferior because of their physiques.

Every girl should understand that many qualities—physical, intellectual, and social—make her unique, and every attempt should be made to offset any perception that she is somehow "different" and therefore an easy target. Adults can also discuss strategies to combat media messages that accentuate the bodies of girls but not boys, and although many fathers shy away from topics related to their daughters' sexuality, their input, even if indirect, is important. Conveying respect for women who are intelligent and strong, as well as refusing to reinforce any behavior that encourages girls to use their looks to compete with one another, will help convince girls that they are more than just bodies.

Accent on Attitude

At all ages, a person who is positive and confident will be an attractive friend and partner. This is not only common sense but the consensus of experts on *attribution training,* or how we help children *explain* behavior, meaning adults should promote a focus on the aggressor in a constructive way, perhaps considering the recent struggles her tormentor may be experiencing. A "benign" attribution can be substituted for a "hostile" attribution, which may help your girl resolve the social situation in a constructive way and protect her from the vicious cycle of revenge. It is beneficial to deliberately sensitize girls to be forgiving and accepting, while at the same time helping them to maintain a sense of self-esteem and confidence.

Hearing this message over and over again from many different sources (parents, teachers, relatives) helps girls internalize values of competency and caring. Girls can also be encouraged to look for and celebrate the good in others and to build on common interests rather than divide over differences.

It's also important to have a positive attitude yourself and to impart a sense of excitement about adolescence to both your girl and her friends. It's easy to be overwhelmed by the possibility of problems and to forget that this time of discovery and new freedoms can be one of the most creative phases of life. Talk about the fun of friends and the new opportunities for relationships she'll have during her growing years.

Develop Personal Power

Girls who develop confidence through their academic or athletic skills have a sense of self-esteem that is independent from peers and can't be destroyed by situations like RA. Studies have even shown that the better a girl feels about herself, the less likely she is to participate in RA. Finding one or two things she likes and promoting her ability to develop these into a real talent will be more likely to create a lasting, healthy self-esteem than immersing her in so many activities that she doesn't have time to enjoy any.

While she should be able to select the activities she feels most passionate about, adults should be mindful of what they support and pay for. Some sports seem to foster an unhealthy degree of competition, perhaps because of their focus on individual rather than team performance. Many girls believe swimming creates a dynamic ripe for RA: too much time in bathing suits or in locker rooms where bodies are displayed and too much emphasis on individual events and times. Dancing is another activity often identified with RA, perhaps for the same reasons. For girls with floundering self-esteem, an activity with a team or group focus may be a better option.

In addition to school-related clubs or sports, there are programs available that build self-esteem and confidence. Some examples are the Girl Scouts, 4-H clubs, Volunteens, and the Boys and Girls Clubs of America. For adults wanting to learn more about ways to promote integrity, self-esteem, and resiliency in children of all ages, the Search Institute, an independent, nonprofit, nonsectarian organization founded in 1990, is another resource. Known for its Healthy Communities initiatives, Search also has a mission of promoting the well-being of adolescents and children. Much of their work is built on their analysis of forty developmental assets, the "positive experiences, relationships, opportunities, and personal qualities that young people need to grow up healthy, caring, and responsible." (Check www.search-institute.org for more information.)

Having one or two interests outside of school can be a way for girls to meet a variety of friends and to avoid boredom, which has been listed as a frequent reason for starting rumors, gossiping, or creating RA dramas. A mother of five teenage girls says, "I've always exposed them to a wide variety of friends in a wide variety of ages. They had older friends at church, adult friends through their volunteer work, younger friends at family gatherings, and all different sports teams. Even if they did feel unpopular in one place, there was always somewhere else where they were popular."

Connecting a girl with others is a strong protective factor. These others don't necessarily have to be within the immediate family, nor do they have to come from an intact set of parents. Links to extended relatives, volunteer projects, community organizations, and faith communities will all give her different perspectives and provide a richer database of resources for her to draw on in times of trouble.

Another way to promote a girl's sense of personal power is to prepare her for situations involving RA. We know that every girl has been in the role of a bystander at some point in her life, meaning she has stood by while an aggressive girl abused a victim. Talk to your girl about these situations. What are her options? What is expected? What is important? Emphasize that there is no such thing as a middle ground: either you are for RA or against RA. If you take no action, you signal to others that their behavior is acceptable and reinforce the aggressor. These ideas are easy to talk about but much harder to put into practice when the situation arises. Encourage her to role-play possible situations she may encounter or to rehearse statements to herself in the mirror.

Involved but Unobtrusive

Adolescence is a time when parental involvement takes on a different flavor, since the people girls most want to be involved with are those their own age. However, girls suggest that there are still plenty of ways for adults to stay connected: providing space for parties and gatherings; buying food; helping with transportation; being part of sports teams or clubs, whether by coaching, teaching, or helping with fund-raising; chaperoning on trips; volunteering to speak to school classes (you may have to pick ones she is not part of); and joining groups attended by other parents of children her age. Your goal is to understand her world. Connecting with it in any capacity will help you appreciate the lived experience of teenage girls. You might even volunteer to mentor or tutor other girls her age or help supervise an activity she isn't involved in, if she objects too strongly to your presence.

You can achieve more direct, everyday connections by watching television shows she likes with her or knowing who her "real" friends are and what she likes to do on a free afternoon. Establish one ritual that will not be compromised, whether that is meals together, ten minutes at bedtime to discuss her day, a telephone call to touch base when she comes home from school, or breakfast out on Saturday mornings. One mother makes a point of gathering her three daughters together when they come home from school, sprawling out on her king-sized bed, and talking about the events of the day for twenty minutes. The earlier you set up this routine, the more she will consider it a good and expected and valued part of her life.

Be involved with her friends too. Obviously you aren't going to join them in shopping outings or turn their trip to the movies into a threesome, but research suggests that the best predictor of whether or not an adolescent engages in destructive behavior is her *friends'* destructive behavior. Get a sense of what the girls she spends the most time with are like, and make it more convenient for her to be with peers who are a good influence. At younger ages, tactful supervision and input to groups of girls are also critical components in reducing RA. Redirecting ("Who wants to go to the mall?") or distracting ("It's snack time!") when behavior turns aggressive can be less obtrusive ways to get involved, but don't hesitate to offer to drive girls home if they don't respond to your input.

Moral Guidance

While teens in general are at a stage in life when they may begin to question religious traditions and values they have been brought up with, a sense of spirituality is a powerful protective factor. One recent study showed that girls who were unsure about their moral identity were more likely to be aggressors. Framing RA in a moral context—as behavior that hurts and even damages another person—will help reverse the beliefs that gossip, rumors, and RA dramas are "fun" or "just something to do," as some girls have suggested.

As one teacher observes, adolescence is a prime time to give students a moral framework of kindness: "We do a lot of relational things, especially in middle school. We have changed our curriculum, where we are now doing six-week programs, one on relationships, one on morality, one on conscience, one on hurting and healing. That was the one that was powerful this year because of 9/11. It sort of brought real life into their spirituality. They can learn all of this stuff in their head, but they don't learn how to use it in life, and what good is it?

Catch her being kind and comment on it. Praising her for being considerate will get you a lot further than criticizing her for gossiping about a friend. Talk about specific ways she (and you) can help others and plan activities that will put these ideas into action. This is an area where all adults can participate: moms, dads, coaches, religious educators, and other relatives can all take responsibility for including girls in "kindness days" or "service days," special days set aside for helping others.

Follow through on these one-day events with a daily reminder. One mom encourages her daughter to draw less popular girls into her group. Another mom asks her daughter at the end of each day, "Who did you help today?"

The following story shows how one girl learned the importance of being true to yourself and the values you believe in.

FRESH START

The first year in high school was a year of lessons in life and friendship. When we started our classes, I was pretty uncomfortable, since I was the only one among my group of friends in that class. Then Sandy approached me and we became good friends.

One day she told me that she liked Matt, this guy in our class. Since the guy was my classmate, I tried hooking them up. All three of us became good friends and would always hang out together. Everything was great. When a row started between Matt and me, everything changed for the worse.

I started shouting at him, even though I knew it was wrong. When we patched things up, we found out that lies were told by Sandy to prevent us from being friends again. He ignored her and started hanging with me and our other friends in the higher grades. Everyone blamed me for isolating Sandy and branded me a flirt.

I would go to school late and come home early every day to prevent them from harassing me. Days, weeks, maybe even months passed by without anyone talking to me. I was even afraid of going out of our room in fear that everyone would stare and laugh at me. I felt so depressed and alone. I often cried myself to sleep and wondered why it was happening to me. Most of the people who I thought were my friends abandoned me. There were times when I would walk near her group of friends and they would start whispering, rolling their eyes, or saying rude things to me. There was even a point where I started thinking of killing myself.

My *real* friends gave me the courage to stand up for myself and stop caring what others thought of me. When they noticed that I never went out of our classroom, they asked me what was wrong. I thanked God for giving me friends that did not believe in rumors.

I learned that we must not judge people by how they look or act but by how they interact with you. We must not do the things we think are wrong for the sake of popularity. Also that we must not do things we do not want done to us. And if, right now or in the future, this situation happens to you too, just remember to keep your head up high and go with the people that you can really count on. Their friendship will help you get through whatever you are going through.

—L.M., age 13, Manila, Philippines

Even as adults, some women continue to relate to one another in the same ways that were so damaging during adolescence. At a recent seminar, every hand in the room went up when attendees were asked if they had recently experienced relational aggression in their work or personal lives. The examples they cited were very similar to those of young girls: gossip, undermining, exclusion, targeting, humiliation, and so on. Clearly RA is a learned behavior rather than a developmental phase.

Girls need to see their mothers, teachers, and other adult women interacting in positive ways—living the "confident kindness" principle in everyday life. Tell your daughter about your friends and how much you value them. Share stories of times when women friends supported you in ways that a man could not. Let her hear you give your friends compliments and monitor what she hears you talk about, especially gossip.

Mary Baird, executive director of the Ophelia Project, mother of a teenage daughter, and a psychiatric nurse specialist, says that girls tell her they have never learned these kinds of friendship skills in school. "This is so important!" she emphasizes. "Beginning in elementary school, girls need to learn to think about what makes a good friend, how do you keep a friend, all those things. I do an activity with girls where I stand up and talk about a beautiful necklace I have that I really love, and I ask them what they think I do to take care of it. They say, 'Treat it gently,' 'Take it off at night so it won't get broken,' and so on. Then I make the point that they need to take care of their friendships in the same way."

Other adults are important in this regard. Girls need to see their female teachers, administrators, and coaches as well as other adult women in their lives support one another. Fathers and other males who are influential to a girl also need to monitor how their actions may be perceived. Dads who role-model openly aggressive behavior in their work and personal lives, coaches who emphasize toughness rather than teamwork, and adults who compete rather than cooperate give girls subtle messages that these behaviors are acceptable.

Parenting Ages and Stages

In addition to preparing girls for each new phase of life, parents need to prepare themselves. Middle school is a special challenge because daughters begin to move toward a more independent lifestyle. Just as a daughter shifts her focus to peers, parents must surrender a bit of their control and allow new freedoms.

"I often believe that the parents who are best during kindergarten through sixth grade are the very worst during middle school and high school," a family therapist and mother of a teenage girl comments. "Think about it. When children are younger, you are choosing their clothes, packing their lunches, getting them to activities, helping organize homework. It's all about control. When middle school comes, suddenly a girl needs to do these things for herself, and it's really hard for some parents, moms in particular, to change their style. They want to hang on to that elementary school approach to mothering."

No matter what the girl's age, adults need to address RA dramas that have spiraled out of control. Consider the story of Lisa, who at nineteen still becomes emotional when she remembers witnessing the continual harassment of Mia, an obese girl who moved into her school district during ninth grade.

"I was never brave enough to stand up and defend Mia, but in my mind I cringed every time the ridicule started. Sometimes I even had tears in my eyes when my friends would make fun of her, but I was scared to speak up. My weight wasn't ideal either, and I was afraid they'd turn on me next." Lisa shakes her head sadly when sharing this tale. "I still wonder about Mia and what happened to her. I wish I could let her know the meanness wasn't really about her. My friends did it to someone else the year before she moved in, for no reason at all."

In this type of scenario, adults need to collaborate with daughters to develop a joint solution, keeping in mind that whether your girl is victim, aggressor, or bystander, the residual effects can be dramatic. Encourage the Lisas of this world to come up with a better plan for situations involving hurt to another girl and empower the Mias to take action on their own behalf. If your daughter is the aggressor, try a role reversal where she plays the victim or bystander. As girls mature, they need to know that adults not only believe in their ability to carry out these behaviors with increasing independence, they expect them to.

As girls mature, parents need to adjust their involvement in other domains of their daughters' lives. While it's appropriate to actively participate in a child's life during the elementary school years, the means of participation change in the middle and high school years. Being aware of school policies, attending meetings, talking with other parents, and staying in touch with teachers are all constants, but they play out differently. Increasingly, a girl will want and need to be empowered to act on her own behalf and to learn how to access resources in the school system for herself. One therapist likens this time to the toddler years, when exploring new environments is exciting as long as it's possible to return to Mom's side whenever the newly independent child chooses to. Adolescent girls should also feel free to explore within safe limits, knowing that moms, dads, and others are available for emotional support as needed.

GIVE GIRLS THE COURAGE TO BE KIND

It's like we just keep bombarding these girls with the messages and telling them over and over, "Come on, guys, do the right thing!"
—MIDDLE SCHOOL PRINCIPAL

Like any virtue, kindness is a behavior that can be cultivated and rewarded by parents and significant others. Never underestimate the power that you have to influence your girl. Use the following strategies to teach her about friendship skills.

The Ages and Stages of Relationships

While most middle schools offer an orientation in which girls are shown down hallways and through classrooms, the emotional turf they will soon traipse in is often overlooked. The uncertainties—who will I eat lunch with, who will I sit next to in class, and where can I turn for guidance when I get lost?—can be frightening when the security of elementary school is replaced by new freedoms and new demands.

In the same way, when girls enter puberty, we often think we have prepared them by requiring a health class that covers biological processes while never making mention of the emotional issues that accompany puberty. If this topic is not covered in the elementary or middle school your daughter attends, volunteer to find a guest speaker who will visit to discuss the subject. And have conversations about it at home.

Girls also need to know that in late elementary school and in middle school, friendships become all-important. In addition to celebrating the fun that girls can have together as they begin to meet independently from parents and teachers, discuss potential problems. This is a time when RA behaviors peak; often interest in boys can lead to conflict between girls. Romantic relationships are one more way in which girls use social channels to explore their emerging identity. Words of wisdom from adults may not make an immediate impact, but they do make an impression, as demonstrated by the following story.

WHISPERS

My mother warned me! She said, "Mary, be careful of the he-said-she-said-whisper-in-your-ear people in life. You know the ones, they say things like, 'Hey, Mary, did you hear that . . . blah blah blah . . . And oh, I thought you ought to know *because* . . . We are best friends after all, aren't we?'"

I didn't really pay attention to her, but before long I found myself right in the middle of the he-said-she-said crowd, and I have to admit, I liked it. Being popular was fun!

I was surprised too. You would think something as important as becoming popular would take decades. But it didn't!

Mom always said "Things that are cheap and easy won't take long. French fries take about a minute." I guess I forgot about that when I was trying to be cool.

Anyway, in about a week I sounded just like them, dressed like them, and fixed my hair just like them. I was amazing! I was even starting to say the whisper-in-your-ear things.

Mom knew I was turning into one of them, but she let me try it for a while, to see how it felt. I knew deep inside that it never felt quite right to be talking about others in a whisper-in-your-ear sort of way. Besides, my *real* best friend Melinda said I *was* one of them now, not one of her. She said I sounded like them, looked like them, and even *smelled* like them!

She looked so sad too, when stupid Sally said I said nasty things about her, which I didn't! But she says it's too late, I must have, because all the kids knew her secret, and besides, I *knew* deep down inside I was guilty of something. I mean I did sound like, look like, and yes, even smell like them!

I didn't know if being popular was worth it. Not if it hurt friends like Melinda.

When I finally told Mom what had happened, she just shook her head and said, "See, *those* are the he-said-she-said-whisper-in-your-ear ones I'm warning you about. People who throughout life you need to beware of, because they may act like, seem like—but I guarantee they aren't—friends who care!"

And I guess she's right, because when I stopped whispering in other kids' ears, they stopped whispering in mine.

That's okay, though, because my *real* best friend Melinda and I had our ears pierced yesterday and have decided we can't whisper in them anyway. We'll just yell and let everyone know what we're talking about!

—Mary Louise Lynch Santacaterina, United Kingdom

Girls' values about friendship often change as they mature. Popularity seems to change too; the qualities that draw girls to someone in seventh grade are dramatically different from the ones that make someone likable as a high school junior. The expression "People come into our lives for a reason, a season, or a lifetime" is especially true during the teen years. Friendships are incredibly elastic during this time, stretching in all different directions.

Take every opportunity to discuss how friendships change throughout the school years, citing examples from previous years. Construct a "friendship history" that helps your daughter see how other friends have come in and out of her life; do the same for yourself and share the results. Have her tell you what qualities make someone her friend now as compared with in kindergarten, and get as many adults as possible to share how the friends they have now differ or resemble ones they had in high school.

The Friendship Barometer

Your girl can learn to gauge a friendship on the mutual give-and-take all relationships involve. Discuss what makes a good friend; each girl will have her own criteria, but you can help differentiate beneficial as well as destructive aspects of friendship, using examples from her life. Then have her use the friendship barometer to apply these values to her life. For example, if she lists loyalty as one of the things she looks for, you might ask her how she would rate her various friends on a scale of one to ten, ten being the most loyal.

It's also important for her to think about qualities she possesses that make her a friend to others. Help her to be realistic about her own strengths. A girl who states that "Nobody likes me!" or "I don't have any friends!" needs to talk more about what she sees when she looks in the mirror each morning. With guidance, she can learn to examine her beliefs about both herself and the world around her and ask herself how she rates on the friendship barometer. Sometimes books and movies provide an excellent neutral opportunity to discuss these issues. A few resources for this purpose have been listed in Appendix A.

You might also discuss why she thinks certain girls are popular and whether these are qualities she values in a relationship, or have her write or imagine a job description for a friend. What would she look for and how would she decide when someone wasn't a friend? Do the same yourself and identify women who have filled this role in your life.

The Best Friend

Best friends seem especially important to girls during middle school because, in the words of one older girl, "They're like a security blanket during a time when everything is changing and different." Even if a girl has many friends, the lack of a single close pal with whom she can share her deepest secrets can leave her feeling dissatisfied, empty, and unpopular.

One girl, now a senior in high school, explains, "Girls can do mean things, especially in middle school, which is a time of high insecurity. Girls have rigid rules then; they need to be with a certain group and need to know certain girls are their friends or not. It's important to have a best friend because you know that person can be counted on. During middle school some of the girls hung around with each other and then separated; the potential to be mean to each other existed during those times of separation. Now they can be apart from each other but still be close. You realize you can have different friends for different things."

Another older girl says, "Actually, there was a group of four of us, and two of us were like really, really close and the other two girls were like really, really close. But we would, all four of us, kind of just be friends. Sometimes when we went on field trips, you had to pick a partner to ride on the bus with and to hang around with the whole entire day. And I remember one time I wanted to be partners with one girl, who was my best friend at that time, and she didn't want to be my partner. I got really upset because I didn't want to be stuck with the other girl, even though she was my good friend too. I ended up spending the entire day with the girl I didn't want to be with, and we had so much fun. I kind of got forced into the situation, but we ended up having a great time on the field trip and we are best friends today. And the other two girls I am still friends with, but I don't call them up every weekend and say do you want to hang out like I do her."

Even more important than being part of a crowd is having a "best friend." This desire for exclusivity gathers steam in the younger years and peaks during middle school. With threesomes there is always the potential for one girl to be excluded, because, of course, at that time in life, each girl can have only one best friend.

Sometimes, though, the price paid for having a best friend is heavy: being controlled, acting a certain way because the friend dictates it, or excluding others. Later, when a girl looks back, she can often shake her head at the unhealthy dynamics of such a relationship. At the time it is happening, it's hard to be logical.

Cindy, now a senior in high school, recalls going through a phase in middle school when she was friends with Lisa, who demanded that she not associate with other girls. Cindy accepted this behavior because of her perception that Lisa was the most popular girl in their class, and because she was desperate for a best friend. "I would have done anything to be friends with Lisa. At the time, I thought I was lucky to be the one she had chosen! Every morning she would decide how we would spend the day: who we would eat lunch with, which other girls we would be mean to, and what we would do after school. I always went along with whatever she told me."

While Cindy recognized even at the time that it was an unhealthy relationship ("I cried every day that year because of her"), she felt trapped, afraid that if she stood up to Lisa or tried to break things off, life would only become worse. "Everyone recognized how mean she was to me: teachers, my parents, even me, in a way," she says. When her mom encouraged her to seek out other girls and to cool things off with Lisa, Cindy listened but found it hard to take action.

Eventually, summer vacation naturally ended Cindy's close contact with Lisa, who spent time in another state with her family. Through camp and sports Cindy met new girls and began to realize what had happened to her during the past school year. When eighth grade started, she was relieved to find that Lisa wasn't in any of her classes. The relationship gradually dissolved, and now Cindy has gone on to become student council president, while Lisa, once the most popular girl in middle school, is no longer the center of attention.

Still Cindy, who hopes to become a teacher and help other girls master such situations, is grateful for the experience. "I realize how I *don't* want to be," she shares. "For the rest of my life, I'll remember how things were with Lisa and how bad it felt to be so mean to other people just because she told me to."

And what about that need for a "best" friend that led her to do things she wouldn't have on her own? "I have lots of friends now," Cindy answers. "I realize it's better to have a lot of really good friends than a single best friend like Lisa."

Accountability

Don't hesitate to call your daughter and her friends on behaviors that are relationally aggressive. (Encourage her to catch you in the act too, then be careful she doesn't!) You can do it with a touch of humor, using the concept of alerting the "gossip police" or pretending to sound a "rumor alarm." Left on their own, girls do not have the maturity or motivation to monitor such behavior, which is why boredom so often leads to RA.

Training such as the Ophelia Project offers can also give a young woman insight into the need to be accountable for her behavior. In the words of one mentor, "At times it really got to me, because I wanted to watch every word I said and make sure I was a good role model."

Another mentor recalls, "I was at one of my volleyball programs and one of the girls was talking about another girl who is one of my friends. She was talking about how she was playing, and then I was like, 'You know, she is a really nice person, regardless of how she plays volleyball.' And then the girls started to switch tones from ragging on her to saying things like, 'She always does her best on the court.'

"I go through that sometimes at my lunch table. Other girls will tease about some girl and talk about her, and I will say, 'Come on now. You guys know that I am part of the Ophelia Project and I don't want to hear that. Talk about it on your own time.' And they actually stop talking about it because they know I don't stand for it and don't appreciate it."

Consider these thoughts, by middle school teacher Dorothy Strang:

> The capacity for betrayal is not in them but in us, if we leave girls alone when their relational games turn hurtful. Perhaps it is acceptable to let boys work it out with swift arguments and fists, but it is not acceptable to let girls work it out with whispered secrets, he-said-she-said rumors, and hurt feelings stockpiled as social capital. Unchecked, these relational games may become strategies that persist into adulthood.
>
> Many years ago, at a conference in Cleveland where Carol Gilligan first announced her Laurel School findings about the disappearing voice of adolescent (white) girls, psychologist Carlotta Miles remarked that the relational games of girls (black and white) are crucial to the development of their egos and that helping them reach closure on relational issues before adolescence might help reduce the amount of manipulation and fantasizing we find in adult women. Her comment stayed with me as I began working intentionally with girls in my classroom, and I came to realize that she was, like

Gilligan, urging me to look not at what is wrong with girls (their meanness) but to look at what is right about their relational games, to look beyond the troublesome surface of excluding and hurting to what girls are working at, trying to figure out and get right.

It is not innate meanness they are perfecting. It is not the hurtfulness of cliques and the unfairness of social status they are honing. They are working at a much deeper level, at how to *connect* with others. Their early adolescent struggles to make and maintain friendships prefigure all relationships they will forge as maturing and mature women who must make difficult distinctions between companion, colleague, teammate, playmate, friend, confidante.

Keeping these words in mind, be aware that a girl may alienate or aggress against peers who threaten her ability to connect with others. Bring your girl back to a point of feeling confident about her own ability to be a friend and encourage her to link with others in ways that are kind rather than cruel.

RA Alerts

As the number of transitions and changes in a girl's life increases, so does the risk of adjustment problems. Girls face the challenge of navigating middle school while many are simultaneously trying to adjust to the physical changes of puberty. Add to the equation a move to a new school or community, and suddenly the challenges of being an adolescent can feel overwhelming.

When girls are under stress, RA behaviors are likely to escalate. The entry into middle school, with all the changes that this milestone entails, can precipitate aggressive and hurtful behaviors as girls jockey for position. Monitor your girl's life for increased aggression whenever there is more overt competition between girls than usual: when they want a boy's attention, when they try out for a team or school activity, when they anticipate a school dance, or when they run for student government. These are all RA alert times when you may want to check in with her a little more closely about how she's doing. Encourage her to talk with you about why girls might respond in unhealthy ways during these times and brainstorm strategies to deal with the possibility.

RA behaviors also escalate when a new girl moves into the school system. Often, as the newcomer is scrutinized by the old-timers, she may feel judged and rejected. Her response to this perception can lead to such labels as "snob" or "stuck-up." It's easy to see how conflict can build on both sides. The following poem illustrates this situation dramatically.

The New Girl

Pock-faced Liz hunkered behind me
in English class.
She'd snicker at my hair, rant to tall
blond Deirdre beside her: Check out the nest,
the matted tangle at the back of my head
I'd given up trying to be free.
So I chopped it off, never dreaming
the gaping emptiness
glaring off my neck,
never dreaming I'd seek the back stairwell,
eat my cheese sandwich, my bag of chips
in a bathroom stall that barely contained me,
gag of Marlboro smoke in my throat
as the girls traded secrets aloud, the air,
clogged with their confidence,
I tried hard to be still, to silence
the wrapper's deadly crinkle
that would give it all away.

—Andrea Potos, Wisconsin

Before interpreting the behavior of others as aggressive or excluding, both established students and new ones need to validate their perceptions. Giving others the benefit of the doubt is always a good principle for girls who feel a bit insecure during their first days and weeks at a new school. At the same time, making newcomers feel welcome is an important role for entrenched students. Here are some tips from middle school girls who have all moved into new school systems on how to make the move less stressful:

I just smile and say hello to new girls, 'cause that meant a lot to me.

—Shantea, age 11

I invite a new girl to sit at our lunch table so she doesn't have to eat alone.

—Erika, age 12

Give her a tour of the school so she can find her way around.

—Jasmine, age 12

Wear an outfit that gives you confidence on your first day of school.

—Maria, age 13

Ask someone ahead of time if you can eat lunch with them.

—Tamika, age 12

Build Self-Confidence and Self-Esteem

Oddly enough, girls who are aggressive lack self-confidence. While to others a girl may seem to be the busy "Queen Bee" who buzzes furiously from crowd to crowd, in reality a girl who aggressively manipulates others does so because she lacks confidence in her own abilities. Just as much as victims and bystanders, bullies need to be encouraged to develop inner strength and confidence.

As one therapist summarizes it, "The kid who lashes out is really scared to death underneath, afraid she will be attacked first. It's so obvious to any adult, but her friends don't see it. The witnesses and victims are scared too, so fear is the operating principle here. Girls need to develop confidence in themselves to overcome this." They may not talk about "self-confidence" in relation to problem situations at school; girls need help to make the connection. Encourage your girl to explore what makes her feel good about herself, either through simple discussion or deliberate activities, such as a Sunday school or other class on powerful women. Ask girls to identify women they consider strong and positive role models and to specify why. Games such as the PowHer Game for Girls (see Appendix B) can also help explore these issues.

Teach Assertive (Not Aggressive) Communication

Too often, the words *assertive* and *aggressive* are used interchangeably, without a clear understanding of the difference between these two ways of communicating. *Assertive* means expressing your opinions, feelings, attitudes, and rights in a manner that doesn't take advantage of other people or hurt their feelings. *Aggressive* means getting your needs met at the expense of others; bullies communicate in aggressive, hurtful ways. Passive behavior is failing to speak up when you want to because of a lack of courage or ability.

The basic format for assertive communication involves three steps. First, validate the other person by recognizing how she's feeling or what she's done. Second, state your feelings about the behavior. Third, make a request for change or tell the other person what you would like.

Think of the formula as "When you do . . ." plus "I feel . . ." plus "I would like you to . . ." For instance, "When you stop talking to me, it really hurts my feelings. I'd like you to tell me to my face why you're upset with me."

Middle school guidance counselor and GENAustin board member Carolyn Brooks uses a technique she learned called "sandwiching" to help girls with assertiveness. She explains, "I tell the girls to put the so-called negative statement in between two positive ones. They might say, 'I really value your friendship, but I don't like it when you make fun of my clothes. I really want to keep being your friend, so can we try to work something out?'" In this way, girls learn to express their feelings without hurting another.

This following story demonstrates how one girl used an abbreviated assertiveness approach to deal with aggression.

I AM . . .

I got elected to be the freshman representative to our dance team even though I wasn't the most popular girl in my class. One day totally out of the blue, a girl who was jealous of this yelled at me from across the hall at school, "Hey, Sarah, come here!" So I go over there and she says she heard that I wanted her boyfriend. My friend, who was with me, just kind of snapped at her, "*You* have a boyfriend?"

It was funny, but it didn't exactly help the situation. I said, "I don't even know who your boyfriend is. Besides, I gotta go to class." I walked away and just let her stand there. She sent someone after me into my classroom with a note saying to meet her at the door after class. I wasn't too worried, but just to be safe I told the teacher. I wanted to make sure someone knew, so I wouldn't get in any trouble if things heated up. The teacher advised me to stick close to my friends for a while, when I was in the hallway or in the bathroom.

This went on for several days. After every lunch there she was, threatening to beat me up. And every day I told the teacher.

One day she said, "I heard you are trashing me, that's what Linda said."

"Well, let's go get Linda and talk to her about it," I responded.

"No!" she yelled. "I want to settle this right here and right now!" I wouldn't give in, so she yelled, "Who the f—— do you think you are?"

I calmly responded, "I am Sarah Wyse and who are you?" and then I walked away.

She wanted to beat me up physically, but my words and passive reaction stopped her. The teacher I had kept informed had sent an anonymous referral to the guidance counselor and obviously it worked!

—Sarah Annamarie Wyse, age 15, Michigan

Strategies 4–7:
CONFRONT RA

BEGIN WITH THE FIRST HURTS

At first I didn't have any idea what relational aggression was, but then the more I heard, the more I thought about girls at my school and I was, like, Oh yeah, this fits.
—CAMP OPHELIA SENIOR COUNSELOR

Even the best efforts to build a girl's sense of inner safety and confidence can be undone when she finds herself in unfamiliar physical or emotional territory, and the finest friendship skills are no insurance that RA will never impact on her life. There will always be other girls who feel insecure and threatened by others and respond in an aggressive way. Even the earliest, mildest episodes of RA need to be dealt with promptly and effectively. If your girl comes home from time to time with complaints of either being victimized or seeing another girl hurt (aggressors rarely realize their behavior is at fault), keep these principles in mind.

Step in Early
Take action to squelch problem behaviors before they escalate into overt RA that affects entire groups of girls. You can do this by stressing shared responsibility communicating clear behavioral expectations, and having children make a com mitment to kindness ahead of time, as demonstrated by the

following story, shared by a religious education teacher from California:

> We have a respect contract that is signed by the student and parent of every child in the program from grade one through eight. The middle school seventh- and eighth-grade respect contract is a little more detailed, because we had gotten into some problems. But it's the best thing that I've found—it's like a principle kind of thing—and if somebody in the office can pull up that little respect contract and the teacher tells us what has happened, we can say, "Right here you said that you would respect and listen to people in the classroom and give them their chance to talk. You signed up right there," and the consequences are right there.
>
> The consequences are in steps. The first time the child just talks to me. The second time the child comes to me, a phone call is made to the parents. Usually that's as far as we have to go, because the parents are great. They are there. They want their kids to do well. The third time the child is released for a period of time. The child has to be home-schooled or the parent has to come into the classroom and sit.
>
> We had an incident where one of the two parents had to come, and the dad had work to do, but he wanted the kid there, so he brought in his laptop and he was doing his work in the back of the class. It was really interesting.
>
> One teacher even made copies of contracts. She keeps contracts in her classes, and she uses that as a tool right in the classroom. They are sitting in a box on her desk every week.

In an Ophelia Project program, small groups of middle school girls met with older mentors and created behavioral contracts outlining how they would support a victim and take a stand against RA for the next week in school. Everyone signed the agreement, which focused on demonstrating shared concern for the victim. Later the group reconvened to discuss the experience, including how successful they had been and what obstacles they had encountered. One girl commented, "It was easier standing up for the victim when you knew a bunch of other people were doing the same thing, and we all agreed to do it."

Develop Her Anti-RA Skills

Insecurity and fear are fertile ground for growing RA behaviors—inciting aggressors to lash out at others, prohibiting bystanders from getting involved, and keeping victims intimidated into silence. Identifying and celebrating your girl's strengths can make the difference between her being overcome when targeted by RA and her growing stronger, as the following story illustrates.

ISLANDS OF COMPETENCE

I am a clinical social worker in private practice and mother of a ninth-grade daughter who was a victim of bullying. In eighth grade she attended a small school with approximately fifty students in her class. The primary bully was a classmate whose older brother had cancer and died. The girl reportedly was not supposed to talk about her brother's condition with anyone. His illness was kept within the family.

This classmate accused my daughter of saying something about her mother. Rumors spread that my daughter "had done something wrong" and that no one should talk to her or socialize with her. One day three girls called her at the same time to tell her she would no longer be able to be in their group. I can still hear my daughter's voice as she asked if she would eventually be included again, to which they responded, "Not for anytime soon."

Our family had had this group of girls at our house nearly every Friday night for sixth grade and part of seventh grade. Several of them were in our car pool to school and had played soccer with my daughter. One of them had been classmates with my daughter since preschool.

The faculty at school was aware of the situation but felt they couldn't intervene unless they actually witnessed behaviors. Finally a teacher saw the girls bring my daughter into a classroom where she was told she was being disinvited to a birthday party they were all going to, which included a sleepover. The teacher reported the incident to the other faculty.

No one ever called me from the school. I finally called them when another adult asked me if my daughter was all right. The group of girls had been reprimanded; their parents had been called. Only one mother called me to apologize.

I worked hard to stay involved in the mother-daughter philanthropy organization we belonged to, believing contributions there would help with my daughter's sense of self. Our psychiatrist, who had been treating her for AD/HD, put her on an antidepressant. With the help and kindness of her teacher she turned her energies toward schoolwork and did very well. She also put her energies into family and the children she loves to baby-sit for. This has continued to be the focus of her energy, and it's a positive one.

My daughter still has not been able to get involved with

friends outside of school, even though I have tried to find creative ways for this to happen. She continues to be left out. Unfortunately, four of the girls involved in the eighth-grade aggression are at her school now.

My daughter is a wonderful girl, very sweet and kind. She works magic with children and is very responsible. I hope that our family support—providing a safe haven at home, as well as finding "islands of competence" in her to celebrate—will continue to hold her and comfort her as she moves through high school.

—Irene Kennedy, North Carolina

Problem-Solving/ Conflict Resolution Skills

When girls are without the basic skills for peacefully resolving differences, conflicts can easily be blown out of proportion, leading to aggression. The smallest incidents of RA can be used as stimuli for group learning that involves all generations and provides opportunities for sharing creative approaches to solving problems and resolving conflict without aggression. If you communicate well, your entire family might take the opportunity to help your girl to talk out a conflict that involved hurtful behaviors and to work out alternative solutions. Share experiences from your professional or personal life that were similar and challenge her to help you resolve them, thereby giving her practice and empowering her to use her skills gainfully. Practicing and reinforcing these behaviors at home with siblings, parents, or other relatives can give her the confidence to take action in situations involving her peers.

Later organize activities where groups of girls can practice resolving differences without aggression or violence, much as the Ophelia Project and others use role playing in schools. A good approach is to have girls share stories of RA and then explore how problem solving could have been used to deal with the situation. The following story is a painful example of how failure to resolve conflict early on can lead to bigger problems.

THE DEEPEST HURT

I have been through so many years of schooling, but tenth grade has been my hardest. I have always had friends and been the popular girl in school, but this year has been very tough—I have gone through so many friendships, it isn't even funny. A girl, Renae, has been tormenting me since the beginning of the year. She constantly calls me obscene names and talks crap about me.

Renae is kind of a bigger girl, not fat, but bigger than I am. When she first started picking on me, I used to get smart with her, and we would even argue. All my friends kept telling me to ignore her and everything would turn out fine, but I couldn't.

She would see me walking around the school and would say, "Eww, don't hang out with her! You might end up just like her!" Then sometimes my friends would leave me when she was around. I don't exactly remember why she started tormenting me, but it hurts deep down inside because we were like sisters back in eighth grade.

What helps me is my sense of ignoring. I'm pretty used to ignoring people, so I just block her out of my head. I worry about more important things, like school, friends, and family.

I hope that with time she'll realize how badly she hurt me, maybe not outside, but inside. No one should ever go around and start tormenting other people for no reason at all. It's just like the Golden Rule: Do unto others as you would have them do unto you. This means don't hurt anyone else's feelings because you wouldn't appreciate it if someone did the exact same thing to you.

If anyone torments you and calls you inappropriate names, just ignore them. The second thing you can do is go tell someone. If I could take back anything, I would have gone to a higher authority when she first started making fun of me and teasing me. Maybe someday this will pass over, but until it does, Renae will continue walking around and hurting me deep inside.

—Lana G., age 16, Pennsylvania

If an adult had gotten involved and used some basic problem-solving/conflict resolution techniques to help Lana and Renae, the outcome of this situation might have been completely different.

Safe Places, Safe People

Teach your girl to remove herself from situations where harassment is occurring. Any number of places in the school and home environment can be identified as safe, but perhaps having a peer-patrolled space designated as an "aggression-free zone" is a goal schools can strive for. What makes a place safe and sacred is that no one is permitted to judge, tease, or demean another person. In that space, the rules are clear and understood by all. A young woman from the Ophelia Project's Fairview Advisory Council describes a safe place for girls as "a place where you can say anything and not be judged for how you act or what you say."

Identify persons she can turn to for help and brainstorm ways your daughter can respond to her tormentors. She might use humor, for example. One teacher recalls a girl who was being pelted with spitballs; she carefully collected them in a Baggie, suggesting they were just right for her spitball collection.

During the schoolday girls need a safe adult to turn to when problems occur. Again and again girls voice their belief that teachers are not a resource for safety. Some girls say their relationships with teachers are complicated by grade giving, others don't trust that their confidences won't be shared in the teachers' lounge, and still others feel that their teachers either don't care or don't know what to do. Guidance counselors, school nurses, coaches, and other adult relatives or friends can be alternate sources of safety for girls, but teachers should also reexamine how they might be of help too.

Some schools have begun to employ an on-site social worker for the purpose of helping students deal with emotional issues such as RA; if your daughter's school doesn't have one, school nurses, guidance counselors, and coaches are other options. One mother who is also a nurse suggests that a school nurse can be "a facilitator of small-group conflict resolution, since we as girls aren't taught conflict resolution. Also there can be education of parents about self-esteem and positive programming; building up emotional aspects of any child at any age is helpful."

With an open attitude school nurses can help create a safe environment where girls can feel free to seek help. Understanding that while somatic complaints such as headaches and stomachaches are often the identified cause for a visit, emotional upset is frequently the underlying issue, a nurse can open the door for discussions and support. He or she can make referrals for counseling or medical follow-up in the case of persistent problems. Guidance counselors and coaches can fill many of the same roles, provided medical concerns have been ruled out.

The author of the following piece encourages other girls to go to safe adults for help with relationship issues sooner than she did.

OUT OF CONTROL

She told me who I should hang out with, like herself and other people I didn't really want to hang out with. She would ask if I would sit with her, but before I could answer, she would say, "Okay, we'll sit together." I would say nicely, "Can I sit with someone else today?" She wouldn't answer and then sat with me anyway. She was always hurting my feelings. It made me mad because I should be able to hang out with the people I want to. She didn't have many friends because she was so mean. I think she was jealous because I had more friends than her. At the end of last year she told my good friend things about me that weren't true, and she stopped speaking to me for a long time. I think she was probably trying to make me lose my friends. She would smile as our teacher walked by while she pinched or kicked me under the table.

Well, the girl that did all that to me is luckily not in my homeroom this year. But I think that if stuff like this happens to other girls, they should probably tell their parents or someone they think can help them, such as their guidance counselor or teacher.

—K. C., age 10, Pennsylvania

Outside school, most girls identify parents as the preferred source of help, even if they don't always appreciate the efforts of Mom or Dad to be supportive. Other adults, such as religious education teachers or activity leaders, can also offer a safe haven for a girl to vent her emotions and receive help. Sometimes leaving the RA drama behind and spending time with a neutral person—creating art, playing basketball, shopping, or doing any enjoyable activity—provides your girl with a welcome diversion.

Older siblings and other female relatives can also be pulled in to help a girl in the midst of an RA crisis she can't resolve. Even if these other family members don't talk to her directly about her troubles, spending time with them can reinforce her sense of being valued and provide an important resource for helping your child understand herself: recent studies confirm that connections with positive role models act as a protective factor for children. Other women can share their experiences with your girl, and even those who are younger may provide support, as happened in this story.

CUTTING

I've quit school because of how horrible it was. After I moved in elementary school, I became popular but lost it all to a rumor, so I cut myself and got sent away. I came home finally and I thought I was better. Then I started tenth grade and found out I had no friends, for what reason I don't know. At school I was known as a crack whore lesbian slut—even though

I don't do drugs, am still a virgin, and I love guys! It didn't matter, it was because of who I hung out with. I lost my grandfather, and my friend killed himself, and soon I started to cut myself. I went to three different hospitals, with two weeks between each visit. I finally turned to God and quit school and started to work. My mom is a big help; so is my little sister, even though she is a year younger than me. She has been through a lot and is teased a lot for being different. She doesn't care at all, which is why I look up to her so much. Without them I might be dead. Well, if it hadn't been for the girls picking at me, killing all the self-esteem and self-worth I had left, I'd be at school. I would be happy. Everyone thinks words don't hurt and that they are just that—words, when really one word could kill everything somebody had inside. I have a fear of girls and not being accepted. I'd do just about anything to be popular. I have one great friend, plus my sister, and that's all I need. Plus my faith in God is a great help!

—D. J., age 15, Indiana

A senior high girl, who works as a mentor with middle schoolers, says, "We see it all, you know—the quarreling friends—and we try to tell them that there are just some girls that don't like you. When you are younger, it means more to you. When you get into high school, you realize that's who you are and it's better."

Talking ahead of time about people and places that make your girl feel safe will both prepare her and help you understand what things create a sense of security for her. Sometimes a simple item—an angel pin, a fuzzy sweater, or a key ring with a stuffed animal or slogan on it—can give a girl a portable sense of security.

Work Through the Behaviors

The very first time you see your girl involved in aggression in any role, start a dialogue with her about what you observed. In addition to sorting out the roles and motivation, ask her, Who holds the power? Who makes the rules? How could the outcome be changed? What would help a bystander take a stand? Whose responsibility is it to change RA behaviors? Is it okay to stand by and watch, if you don't actively get involved in RA? Breaking down situations will help girls see themselves through the eyes of others and begin to identify ways to change their own behavior. It's fairly easy to talk, though, and much harder to do.

One of the counselors at Camp Ophelia raised this point when campers suggested that they would just refuse to take part in shunning another girl. "Okay, we can all agree that's the right thing to do now," she said. "But when it's *your* friends, and *your* school where this is taking place, how will you really act?" Acknowledging the risks involved in taking a stand, she helped the girls develop a workable plan that had several alternative behaviors. These involved approaching the victim after the aggression had occurred and indicating support, uniting with another bystander and confronting the aggressor, or walking away and refusing to be involved. Role plays are an effective tool to help girls envision themselves in more supportive roles and rewrite the everyday aggressive scripts they confront in their schools and communities.

Girls not only need to be familiar with behaviors that help victims, they need to be encouraged to use them in a variety of contexts. Strategies identified by girls for bystanders include going to stand physically by a victim, challenging the aggressor, ignoring the aggressor, and asking an adult to intervene. (Victims can use many of these same strategies to empower themselves.) Ways to show empathy for the victim are also important, such as writing her a note, inviting her to walk to class with you, or offering to sit next to her in class. It's far easier to make these behaviors a part of her regular repertoire if a girl adopts them early and acts on them in less inflammatory situations.

While the victim or target of aggression is the most natural person to empathize with, bullies and bystanders are hurting inside too. Understanding that insecurity underlies all three RA roles is an insight that will help both adults and girls change the dynamic. Aggressors need to learn to build self-esteem in more effective ways that don't belittle others, while bystanders or girls in the middle need to put their fears aside and develop the courage to take action when RA occurs.

Encourage her to think about enlisting the help of other kids who may not like the girl bullies so much either. There are lots of other girls at her school who are feeling the same way she is. By noticing who the players are in any RA situation, your girl can figure out who might be a valuable ally the next time a problem arises.

It helps if girls who are victims of RA come to understand that not all children feel emotionally secure and that those who do not often bully others. Encourage your daughter to develop empathy for the aggressor, who feels as insecure as the victim she targets. The Ophelia Project uses the analogy of wearing a coat. While the coat is on, what is underneath remains hidden. Sometimes when the coat is removed, the inner "clothing" is surprising. Although these kinds of insights may not remove the hurt of relational aggression, they can help a girl reframe the situation.

When girls are challenged to explain why RA happens, jealousy is almost always the number one reason they give. Prompt your girl to think about what's underneath jealousy, and see if you can help her connect low self-esteem with envying and mistrusting others. The goal is to help her see the connection between feeling threatened and insecure and behavior that manipulates and aggresses against others to build a sense of power.

JEALOUS JEN

My situation began in sixth grade, but its roots began to grow under the surface much earlier than middle school. My close friend Julia began hanging out with Jen. Jen and I were barely acquaintances, but Julia wanted the three of us to become good friends. Soon thereafter Julia discovered that it wasn't going to work. Jen and I are total opposites. Despite our differences, Julia liked spending time with both of us. Optimistic by nature, she never discerned the fact that Jen and I didn't get along.

She couldn't ignore it very long, though. Jen was very insecure. She was mean to a lot of other girls; I never paid attention to why. I wasn't anticipating that she was going to start anything with me. I'm no angel. In fact, like many teen girls I can be straight-up nasty. Due to my quick temper and even quicker mouth, most girls steer clear of a confrontation with me. Jen began to "talk smack" for no apparent reason. She told people that I flirted with her brother and wanted every boy to like me. She told everyone who would listen how I was bossy, stupid, ugly, and a big slut.

At first she denied that she said such things. Finally I got sick of analyzing why she hated me and went into defensive mode. Under the surface, I was also mad that she was spending more and more time with Julia. I shot back with worse insults, mostly just because it was easier for me. As bad as this sounds, it's the truth. I had many friends, got straight A's in school, was pretty athletic, and most people considered me attractive. Jen was a lethargic, vulgar, and loud tomboy with few friends and not good-looking in the least. Julia hated it when I shot my mouth off about her.

Jen and I were both mean to each other. I know the reason I was mean to her. I was young, dumb, and felt a need to defend myself. I can only guess at the reason why she was mean.

Something I didn't see at first, Julia pointed out to me. It was plain old girl-to-girl jealousy. I had so much more going for me, especially in the boy department, which seemed to be a recurring issue.

Was Jen just flat-out mean? I don't think so. Did she act mean because she carried hurt and confusion from childhood experiences with her? It's a good possibility. The truth is that I really don't know, I can only guess.

Jen still hates me to this day, but I pretty much ignore that fact. I'm not fond of her, but I moved on, as making fun of her didn't make me feel good anymore. It didn't make me feel good because I realized that I felt good anyway. I didn't need to make fun of her to feel better about myself. Upon reflection, I almost feel bad for her.

What's the moral of my story? Girls are going to be mean to each other. Human nature makes it inevitable. The smart girls will discover that the trick is to be confident in yourself and be able to do your own thing without worrying about the bitter commentary of others. The unfortunate mean girls will grow up to become mean women. Each girl gets to decide what kind of woman she wants to become.

—Brooke M. Cataldi, an adolescent girl from Pennsylvania

Blaming is counterproductive to healthy development, but processing an RA situation in light of what might motivate other girls to act in certain ways can be a proactive strategy for the future.

Mentoring Works

Match girls the same age with one another and younger girls with older ones. Many successful programs use this approach to give girls a valuable resource they might not otherwise have access to. High school girls have a credibility with middle school girls that moms do not, and middle school girls are more likely to be influential with grade-schoolers.

As one middle school girl describes her mentor, "Betsy was the best. The best part of my schoolday was seeing her. I knew she'd understand how I felt. She was young enough to know what it felt like to have everyone trash you behind your back, but old enough to know how to help me. She's still dealing with RA too, but she helps me see that it's not the end of the world and there are other ways I can deal with it."

Connecting your daughter with older girls, whether through an organized program or an informal mentoring arrangement, will help her frame her experiences with someone who's "been there, done that." Older sisters, cousins, aunts, and family friends who are close to the girl's age can also serve this purpose.

WHEN RA IS SUSTAINED,
AVOID THE BLAME GAME

She was so excited to be invited to the sleepover, since things hadn't been going well with these girls. When I picked her up, she started crying and told me they had locked her out of the house in her pajamas at 3 A.M. I was so mad I almost did a U-turn to go back and scream at the mom for her lack of supervision.

—MOTHER OF A THIRTEEN-YEAR-OLD GIRL

Imagine this scenario: It's mid-September, and the beginning of ninth grade has been rough for your daughter, who is the oldest of your three children and also the most sensitive. Although she is bright and nice-looking, none of her classes this year are with the friends she has been comfortable with since grade school, and each day seems to bring a new problem: another girl makes fun of her clothes or teases her about her lack of interest in boys.

One day you are at home when she gets off the school bus, or you receive a call at work. She is devastated, sobbing so hard she can barely get the words out to tell you that no one would sit with her at lunch.

"No one?" you ask, incredulous.

No one, she confirms, going on to tell you that not only did the girls in her usual crowd physically bar her from eating lunch with them, they informed her she could never again share their table. When she had gone to sit at another table where there was an empty seat, those girls had also slid their trays together and said your daughter wasn't welcome. Consequently she had skipped lunch and gone to the bathroom, where she sat in a stall and cried until it was time for her next class. Of course the other girls noticed her red and puffy eyes and commented on that too.

By now your blood pressure has soared, and your heart is pounding. Your daughter's misery does nothing to soothe your indignation, and your first impulse is to march over to the mothers of the girls who were the first aggressors (you happen to know some of them) and demand not only an apology but an assurance that, from now on, their daughters will welcome your daughter at the lunch table.

Cool Down

Before you say or do anything, take a few deep breaths and calm yourself down. The last thing you want is to get caught up in your own RA drama, calling to accuse or confront other mothers or fathers and passing on secondhand information from your daughter. Therapist Diane Bates-Sier, a licensed social worker involved with bullying programs in several school districts, advises against following your first impulse to intervene. "If you take over and try and 'solve' the problem for your daughter, you automatically convey to her that you don't believe she's strong enough to handle the situation on her own and that you're always going to be the fixer of her problems. Both messages are the wrong ones to send."

So what is a parent or concerned adult to do?

The Victim-Aggressor-Bystander Dynamic

Remember that most girls, like most adult women, have at one time or another been in the roles of victim, bystander, and aggressor. Although in this particular instance your girl is the "wronged" party, she, like every other girl involved, has the capacity to play the roles of bystander and aggressor too. It's also important to keep in mind that all parties involved are hurt by RA, albeit in different ways—even the girl who may appear to be a passive observer. Study after study has documented that each girl—victim, aggressor, and bystander—suffers from involvement in RA. The goal of every adult should be to help girls see alternatives and to promote growth through the situation, rather than to assign blame.

Be a Fact Finder

Force yourself to adopt a nonjudgmental attitude as you listen to her story, and focus on objective details rather than emotions. Girls are very sensitive to the reactions of adults they turn to for advice and comfort. Your response to her will tell her much about how you view her as a person. If you overreact or convey a belief that she is incapable of managing the situation herself, you give her a message that she lacks ability. Help her piece together and process the situation using the following suggestions from Sharon Day, "life coach" and leader of the What Your Daughter Really Wants program.

Sharon believes that parents need to cultivate the attitudes of a coach rather than those of a parent. Her website (www.sharonday.com) talks about training parents to be more like coaches, including such basic skills as how to listen. Life-coaching principles can help an RA victim in the following ways:

1. During emotional times, active listening can be painful, Day concedes, but it is important. Focus on your girl fully, without the distraction of a computer, phone, or house-keeping task.

2. Take off your parent hat, put on your coach hat. Interact from a questioning point of view. Don't ask yes or no

questions; instead ask questions that invite and welcome a fuller response: "What happened next?" "Who said that?" "What did you do?"

3. Listen to the whole story. Get as many details as possible and use those as a way to give your daughter an outlet for expressing her feelings. Sometimes just venting all the details takes away some of the emotional upset.

4. Once she's described all she remembers and talked about how she feels, paraphrase and reflect back what you heard. For example, you might say, "So what I heard is that the other girls refused to let you sit with them, and they said in the future you could never sit with them again?"

5. Give her a hug, and even hold her on your lap if appropriate.

6. Validate. Statements like "Gosh, that had to be horrible," or comments that show you know what she's been through, give her the message that her feelings are legitimate. This is the point when encouragement and motivation to change comes in too. Give her praise. "You're so amazing, being able to express yourself this way" is honest and affirming. Say something with the word *you* in it to show her she has been understood and affirmed.

7. Ask if there's something your daughter can think of to say to those girls. Press a little, and even role-play what she might say to them. Try to get her to come up with something, even if it's "I hate your guts."

8. Try to form her thoughts into a cohesive communication. Ask her to be brave and go say something to them.

Sharon's adolescent daughter had a situation similar to this, and using these steps, she was able to develop a plan to go back and speak to the girls. She returned to tell her mom that things had worked out well.

Based on her work as a life coach and the online seminars she holds with moms, Sharon cautions that if you get sucked into the emotionality of a situation involving RA (as many moms do, having had similar experiences), objectivity often gets lost. Explore the role your girl played in the situation, even if she didn't do anything wrong. Sharon relays a story in which one girl came home very upset and informed her mother she had been bullied. When the mother confronted the "bully," she discovered another side of the story that took away the dynamic of her daughter as victim and more fully explained what had happened. It's better to fill in as many details as you can before responding.

Focus on the Group, Not the Girl

Approach the situation as a group or at least joint problem rather than an individual one, since RA is a *relationship* issue that affects everyone, even the girls who stand by and witness it but don't speak up. Solutions need to be inclusive rather than exclusive. Never single out an aggressor in front of a group and chastise her; she already feels insecure about her ability to be accepted. Instead include the entire group of girls involved, if possible.

Listen Now, Act Later

When an isolated incident occurs, your daughter should be given lots of love and support and encouraged to figure out her own solutions. If the behavior occurs a second or third time, she needs to be pushed to act on her own behalf. When RA persists or is extreme, it's time for you to intervene as her advocate and ally.

Therapist Bates-Sier points out that it rarely works for an adult to take action behind a girl's back. "Involve her. If you're going to contact the school, make sure she knows ahead of time." Given the many stories mothers have shared in which contacting other mothers boomeranged and made aggression worse for their daughters, this is sound advice.

Maintain an Objective Perspective

When you approach teachers, coaches, or other adults, remember to maintain a nonjudgmental attitude, even though your emotions may still be running high. Statements like "You've got a big problem in your classroom," or "Why are you allowing other kids to pick on my daughter?" will start you out in an adversarial stance. Opening with "I've been reading a lot about relational aggression and would like to help figure out ways of creating more positive opportunities for girls in schools," or "There's been so much attention lately to behaviors girls use to hurt one another that I'm concerned. What kinds of situations have you observed with girls hurting other girls on your team?" will put you in a position of advocacy from the start. There's plenty of time to bring up the personal example of your daughter's needs, but beginning with a focus on the big picture is likely to win you more interest and allegiance.

Once the passion of the moment has passed, and perhaps even after your daughter has resolved the situation for herself, you can still work with other adults to prevent recurrences. You will be more effective if you adopt a neutral stance in approaching others about the RA behaviors your daughter has faced.

For example, imagine the telephone rings and you pick it up to hear, "Do you know what your daughter did to my daughter today at lunch? She refused to let her eat at the same table! She even encouraged the other girls to move their trays so my daughter couldn't sit down! Then she said my daughter could *never* eat lunch with them again!"

As compared to: "Hi, this is Theresa, Melanie's mom. I've been thinking of having a group of moms get together to discuss ways we can help our daughters deal with all the changes they're going through in middle school. It seems like right now some girls are having a really tough time in the cafeteria, so I thought having moms meet first might be a good way to share some of the things we've each done to help our daughters."

Using this approach, you've created a way to align yourself with parents, so you can approach them again in the future. Don't be surprised if they aren't as concerned as you about their daughters' behavior; parents of aggressors, and aggressors themselves, rarely see their behavior as bullying. If you wonder about the tendencies of a girl or adult you know, check the quiz "What's Your RA Quotient?" in Appendix C.

Resolve Your Own RA Issues

A school counselor with many years' experience in dealing with middle school girls says she can always tell when a mother has her own "RA baggage." "Something happens to her daughter and bingo, all kinds of memories get triggered, and it's almost like the mom relives her situation. I'll talk to her one minute and the next her daughter will appear in my office using the exact same language. The mom and the daughter are equally upset. It's hard to tell whose needs I should address first."

Part of the reason a national furor over relational aggression has been created may be that we as moms respond from the heart when we hear of girls being hurt. It touches our hearts to think of another young woman being subjected to what we encountered ourselves. Every mom needs to examine her motives, though, and make sure unresolved emotions are not driving her to respond in unproductive ways.

Prevent Conflict from Becoming Physical

The incidence of girl-to-girl physical violence is climbing. Tragically, these physical acts of aggression are preceded by verbal and relational aggression. The example of the young

woman from Williamsport, Pennsylvania, who shot a classmate after being tormented by her is a graphic illustration of
this point, as is the story by Smith about one girl stabbing
another. Verbal aggression must not be allowed to escalate,
because given enough time and intensity, an RA drama can
spiral into physical violence.

SURPRISE ATTACK

The first blow to my cheek was like a dream. I could not
move, as if invisible wires welded my feet to the ground. I
could not think, even by the time the second punch had
landed. I was not born to fight; too scrawny, too gentle, and
very scared.

When I took kung fu classes, my instructors were always
frustrated with my inability to be aggressive. Every class was
the same: "Come on, you can punch harder than the bag.
Alexandra, punch harder . . . harder."

I simply assumed that one day my veins would fill with
superhero madness as I showed the world what I was really
made of. Then there I was. It was the chance to prove my
worth after two years of kung fu, and I could not move a
muscle. She was strong, even from behind, as she fled, leaving
me on those stairs.

After she left, I sat there in shock, all jelly limbs and limp
back.

Why did she hate me? The thought kept coming back in
fuzzy waves. How long had I known her, three or four years? I
couldn't figure out when we had even talked. We were in the

same class, but she had her friends and I had mine. I lived on the hill, she lived in the flats. I took kung fu, and she kicked my ass.

I could not remember anybody else who hated me with such boiling fury. Simple grudges that every girl has—death looks and put-downs and the rest of the hell that we load on each other—in the end it was always the same: my archenemies and I would walk hand in hand, cowboy style, off into the sunset. The beauty of forgiving grows in the most unlikely places.

This was hate. I could not remember hating. Plotting for bruises is just not my way. It did not make sense.

When I got home, I cried. My cheek, though redder than raw steak, hardly hurt.

Mom held me, because that is just what moms do: hold without questioning, deep to the heart.

"Isn't it obvious why?" she said after I cooled down.

"What?" It clearly wasn't obvious to me.

"She's deathly jealous of you."

Jealous of me? That was the response that moms always give to everything.

The stories I made up instead of Mom's reasoning wavered far from reality. It happened because she thought I had given her a nasty look. Or perchance she thought I was somebody else, but that made no sense. Always it came back to what Mom said.

Late at night, weeks after it happened, that afternoon would come back, shadowing my fantasy. I began to wonder what she did after she left me. Had her hand hurt more than my cheek, as if somehow her rage, her anger, and possibly her jealousy had reversed themselves from my cheek, back into her heart, staining her consciousness with its black pain? Is it possible to live with such hate?

—Alexandra Cosima Lewis, Oregon

FRIENDS . . . OR NOT

In sixth grade I was overwhelmed with new freedom. In my small Catholic school, we could change classes and be taught by different teachers. We had lockers and new activities. Many kids had left and new kids arrived.

I met Christie at a swim party, and we clicked right away. When I would go to her house, we were able to walk around alone downtown and take the bus back to her house. These were things I had never been allowed to do.

I remember when things turned ugly. It was lunchtime and Christie had blown up about Val, another girl who was my friend. Val approached me later that day and asked if Christie had been talking behind her back. Without even thinking, I told her yes.

This was the worst mistake I could have made. I was talking to a few of my friends when Christie came up and started screaming at me, accusing me of "backstabbing" her and saying I was not a true friend. She cursed at me and ran away.

Before I could do anything, a rope went around my neck.

Christie had come up behind me, tightened the rope, and pushed me to the ground. I don't know how long this went on, or who was watching it happen, because I was scared and could hardly breathe.

The rest of the day was like a blur. The principal told Christie that my parents could sue her parents and that her actions were not acceptable. She also told Christie she was going to forgive her and not give her a punishment, since it was her first year at the school.

I cried the entire time. When I would say, "I cannot believe you did this to me," she would just start screaming about how her parents were divorced and how she had to start a new school. How she trusted me and I deserved what I had gotten.

I was positive I would never trust Christie again, but somehow or another, we started talking. She told me how sorry she was and how she missed me. She wanted me to come over one weekend, and I accepted. My parents were furious, but I thought they were unfair.

I continued to go to Christie's house, telling my parents I was with other friends. When she was mad at me, she would call me names or say I was stupid. Sometimes she hit me and threw things at me or threatened to kill me or one of my parents. I took it all, because she was the only friend I had left. Eventually everything revolved around Christie. I was so scared to lose her that I would just take her behavior and apologize.

My grades dropped and I wasn't even passing a few classes.

My parents noticed and made me see the school counselor almost every day. Some days I would cry and talk to her about things that were bothering me, but she did not understand about Christie; no one did.

Monica, one of my good friends from earlier years, saw what was happening. She started talking to me and became very reliable and trustworthy. She got adults to try and get me help. With Monica's help I stopped talking to Christie. Things got a lot better after that; my grades improved so that I passed sixth grade (barely). Christie left our school that year.

Now I am in high school. I have seen Christie a few times on the street and was told she has her own band at her high school and is part of every play and production. I'm happy for her.

When I hear about violence and girls hurting other girls, I feel sorry for the girl that is hurting people. I am also more aware of girls helping girls, and I try my hardest to be one of them.

—Lu, age 17, California

ENLIST THE HELP OF OTHERS

So I read this book that said I need to listen to my daughter, but I wonder, how would I know she was having these kinds of problems if I wasn't already listening? And wouldn't I move heaven and earth to change things for her if I could? What's a mom to do?

— MOTHER OF A TWELVE-YEAR-OLD GIRL
VICTIMIZED BY RA

Experts say that adults cannot rush in to remove every hardship from a child's life: "This is a time when your child is struggling to separate from you developmentally. If you remove every obstacle in her way, how will she learn to deal with problems later on?" As for adolescent girls themselves, the consensus is that parents should maintain a hands-off attitude.

"If my mom called up my friend's mom and told her to be nice to me, I'd just die," one teenager shared. "I'd never forgive her for invading my privacy."

Clearly, though, there are times when more active adult intervention is needed: when a girl is unable to resolve situations on her own, when the aggression is prolonged, or when she is clearly suffering from the effects of RA. There are ways to step in when you see depression, truancy, or other signs of fractured self-esteem creeping into a girl's life because of RA.

Don't Hesitate to Get or Provide Help

Deciding when your girl needs you to actively intervene and provide tangible forms of help versus when you should stand back and let her solve problems herself is one of the most challenging tasks a parent faces. The recent message that if mothers just listen a little harder or put forth a little more effort, they can reverse RA may lead many women to believe that they should intervene at all costs. This mistaken advice leads parents to feel that they should be able to handle problems single-handedly; it often results in unnecessary guilt and suffering when their efforts don't work.

In reality, RA is a widespread problem that needs to be tackled by both adults and girls who understand that change is possible. Spreading sensationalized stories of victims and aggressors without offering alternatives for help only condones such behavior and sets up competition for even worse scenarios. No one has to accept these stories as "normal," nor do parents need to blame themselves for not being able to shield their daughters from RA damage. To guide girls in the principle of confident kindness takes a consistent message from the many players in her social life: family, school, peers, and community. Girls also feel secure knowing that, when needed, adults can be counted on to advocate on their behalf.

STEPPING IN

Every day I speak with my children (daughters age eleven, nine, seven, and a son age five) to help them deal with relational aggression. In my eleven years of parenting, I have seen these behaviors begin in preschool, between girl and girl, girl and boy, and boy and boy. Sometimes it is between two individuals or in groups. There is the eye rolling, secret telling, singling out, ignoring, name-calling, threatening, and even physical aggression.

Alannah, my oldest daughter, is quiet (until known), sensitive, kind, thoughtful, and polite. I encourage her to speak up for herself and to turn to the teacher or another adult when she needs help. Most days she is too intimidated to do so.

Amanda and Neva made the entire fourth-grade school year very difficult for Alannah. Alannah was told what to do, where to sit at lunch, and threatened if she didn't do it. Their behavior, which included swearing and talking about gays and lesbians, made my then ten-year-old daughter uncomfortable.

Alannah and I discussed how to cope with the situation or what to do differently the next time. I also spent much time in heartache because my child was pulling her eyelashes out at bedtime from stress. I sought information from various sources, including her pediatrician, and taught her relaxation and behavior modification to deal with the cruelty. All the while I was thinking, "Adolescence hasn't even occurred yet."

One night it was eleven o'clock and I was leaving Alannah's bedside for the third night in a row. One eyelid maybe had five eyelashes left on it. After being the victim since preschool, she voiced anger and told me how she was going to treat them— she would be the aggressor. Wrong!

I went to school the following morning. My daughter and I talked to the teacher, the principal was made aware, and a meeting was held with the girls. Alannah discussed her feelings. We talked to the aggressors about the behavior they had been using all school year.

I learned much from that act. I only wish I had gone earlier.

Some children do need parental involvement to handle situations. I wish I had contacted their parents, and I feel teachers should inform parents. That was never done. I later found out that Alannah was this year's victim, last year it was another girl, and the year before that yet another.

Some girls are more vulnerable than others. My daughters are sensitive, kind people-pleasers much like myself, trying never to hurt someone else's feelings, regardless of their own, and not wanting to bother the teacher.

I am now teaching my children that when a friend is not a friend, it is okay to pull away from that relationship. They should live by the Golden Rule.

—Deborah Labesky, Pennsylvania

Tap into Resources Outside the Family

Of course most moms and dads do listen to their daughters, or else they wouldn't already know that the girls are dealing with and distressed by situations involving RA. Most parents would also do anything humanly possible to reverse the hurt their girl has experienced. So why haven't good parents been enough to make RA go away? The very fact that RA behaviors occur primarily outside the family unit suggests that the dynamics are bigger than any one mother's or father's good intentions.

Keep listening. It never hurts to brush up on your skills and to make sure your girl feels you are really hearing what she has to say. Are you focused on her, with the television, computer, radio, and whatever other distractions may exist in your house temporarily out of the way? Do you check in with her every day to see how she's doing? Can you reserve a block of time that is exclusively hers, every day?

Outside the family, coaches, teachers, and religious leaders can also make an extra effort to bolster your girl's self-esteem. Focus on helping her have positive experiences and provide her with opportunities that will enhance her sense of accomplishment. Interventions don't have to be anything monumental: even an adult's recognizing her for a job well done or taking the time to inquire about her well-being can signal a concern that is surprisingly meaningful to girls.

Shelly Neufer, a track and swim coach for adolescent girls and mom to three kids, ages nine, eleven, and thirteen, describes how she curtails RA among the teams she works with:

There are two other coaches, both women. We get along really well, the coaches and the kids. The beginning of the year we will have the girls coming in saying, "She didn't do what she was supposed to," and "So-and-so wasn't doing whatever," or "So-and-so is being nasty," so I have my own little packet of things that I do with the kids. I give them "The Fence," which is this story: Say there is a child who is always having bad days or is nasty to people. Each time she is negative, she is supposed to go hammer a nail in a fence. Then when she has become pleasant and kind, she can start taking the nails out day by day. When all is said and done, there will still be holes in the fence. That's the way words cut. There is still a hole. You can't say I am sorry and take it back; it's still there.

I don't single any one person out, even if they are in the middle of a problem. I give this to the whole group.

There are other things. There was this one gal who was new, a seventh grader, and she was just kind of by herself. So the first meet she ran, I put her in the relay, and you should have seen her come alive, I mean it was just wonderful. She was all bubbling and excited. And then being on a relay, they have to work on a handout, and so it kind of brings the girls together. They were really good with bringing her in.

She was not up to their ability, but they took her and worked with her. I didn't have to say to them, "Now work with her"; they did it themselves.

Actions speak louder than words. I think if you are a person who lives the way you want them to, they will see and it will rub off. We the coaches get along with each other and when we have to talk about an issue with a child, we don't do it in front of the other kids, we will take that kid aside and have a talk.

Sometimes in sports there's a tendency to focus on the "stars" and give them the most attention. That's a bad message about life in general—that "you have to be *the* best at everything" rather than "you have to learn to work with everyone to achieve a goal," which I think is far more important. Give awards to the person with the most team spirit, or the person who would motivate other people the most, or the person who brought everybody together, because I think those things are just as important as the ribbons.

It's not just about coming in first; it's about being a responsible person. If you are told to do something and it takes you longer to do it but in the end you have done it, that's the thing that counts.

Ask for Advice

Brainstorm with as many people as possible to identify all possible solutions, and benefit from the perspective of others. While most mothers and fathers view their daughters in RA situations as victims, a girl's interpretation of a situation and the information she presents to her parents can be distorted. More than one mother has shared stories of tormented and bullied daughters, only to find out that her daughter instigated or actively participated in the RA behavior.

It's prudent to notice what other daughters are telling their moms and how girls seem to respond to your child. Ask what adults say about her relationships with others. Since few girls are always victims or always aggressors, talking to others can help uncover the truth. (Remember, studies have repeatedly shown that victimized girls are also likely to become aggressors, particularly if they have unresolved feelings of anger and resentment.)

Use the insights you gain to create a list of possible solutions. The approaches you, your girl, and concerned others can generate will be limited only by your creativity. Consider what happened in Warren, Pennsylvania, when parents perceived a problem with RA at their daughters' dance studio and united to work with owner and instructor Linda Dies to develop the RESPECT program (Remember, Everyone, Should be Polite to Everyone and be Caring Too). Girls were encouraged to attach "leaves" to a Tree of Kindness that described caring behaviors they had seen, and extra attention was given to promoting positive dressing-room behaviors and support for younger girls. Within a very short time there was a noticeable improvement in attitudes and a decrease in RA.

Go to the School

You may feel that you don't have the time to visit your girl's school on a regular basis or that your influence alone is not enough to make a change. Connect with other parents. With group effort, a few strategies can make a big difference. One possibility is to draft a policy for zero tolerance of RA behavior, citing examples of other schools that are changing their policies to address more covert forms of aggression.

Enlist the help of teachers, who often have a surprising repertoire of strategies to help girls deal with relationship issues. Here's how one middle school teacher intervened on behalf of a girl in his class:

> I was in physical education, where aggression with the young men was often very easily handled because of its physical nature. The physical challenge was very easy to contain.

It came to a meeting of the minds or fists, and once it was done, it was over. I have had several all-female classes, which were more challenging. Sometimes I knew something was happening but I didn't know why they were doing what they were doing. And quite frankly I am not sure I, as a teacher for the young ladies, did the right things.

One of my strategies was to use activities: in the boys' classes I would use a physical skills challenge, and in the girls' classes I actually taught dance. I had a rather large girl who didn't like gym class, but when we got into dance, she was an excellent dancer. She stepped right up to lead, came right up front and volunteered to teach the class to dance. Her peers were very surprised. She was a new role model.

One thing teachers can do is to listen. I became a better teacher, I think, by listening. I had forgotten that a teacher needs to give students that. Use open-ended discussion, let them talk and be accepted. Don't be judgmental.

I think that boys accept their physical skills and agree on who should be doing what. Bring girls together and they are going to look at who they relate best to. They will interact among themselves better if they know each other.

Teachers are certainly a part of the solution, but they have a complex role with students that can make girls reluctant to approach them for emotional support. Girls say it's difficult to share their deepest hurts with someone who will later be giving them grades for their schoolwork or talking to your aggressors about homework assignments.

It's also not realistic to assign teachers the sole responsibility for solving the RA dilemma when they do not have sole authority over a girl's life. However, it is realistic to offer to work with your child's teachers on classroom strategies, such as activity periods, that can be used as part of the curriculum to teach healthy relationship skills. For example:

A history class can discuss powerful women.

An English class can write about friendships.

A health class can play the PowHer Game for Girls (see
Appendix B).

During activity periods, mentors can work with girls on
collaborative projects or role playing.

A teacher describes her strategies for dealing with RA:

WHY ARE GIRLS SO MEAN?

Emily pauses at the door and looks uneasily around her
English classroom, checking out who is already there and
where they are sitting. In math class there is a seating chart,
but in this class there isn't, so each day she has to decide
where she belongs. Some days Amy waves her over with a
smile, but today Amy's back is turned and she is whispering to
Jane. A bad sign.

Amy is mad at her. Emily runs through the list of her
betrayals: walking to class with Shelley instead of Amy, not
calling last night, wearing the sweater Andy has told Amy
makes Emily look "hot." Jane glances briefly at her, leans
toward Amy, and, laughing, says something behind her hand.

Emily's face flushes. She slides into a seat close to the door
and hunches over her history textbook, hoping Amy and Jane
will think she is studying. Actually, she is planning how best to
tell Shelley about this latest snub.

Scenes like this happen in middle school classrooms every
day. Most teachers consider these social tensions between girls
so ordinary that they pay them no attention, even when

struggles for status and belonging erupt into tears. "Girls will be girls," they sigh in the faculty lounge, at meetings, and even in parent conferences, as if meanness and tears were an inevitable developmental stage. Is this a stage to be humorously deplored or stoically tolerated, a stage that girls will eventually grow out of, if we just leave them alone? Or is it the emergence of fixed and fundamental female traits: meanness, cattiness, deception, manipulation, betrayal?

The tension between Emily and Amy continues to mount. Amy corrals other girls into shunning Emily during the daily preclass ritual of who sits next to whom. For Amy and her friends the key tactic is to get to class early and stake out their desk territory, then to watch Emily scanning the room. As soon as her eyes light on Amy, the girls turn their backs, lean toward one another, and raise one hand to shield their mouths, signaling to Emily that they are talking about her.

Amy and Emily are bright, happy girls and enthusiastic students. At the start of the school year they were "best friends," a crucial distinction for young adolescent girls. They have been in the same class for most of their elementary years, and now the rigors of middle school (changing rooms, teachers, and classmates for every subject) is challenging the foundation of their friendship, just as childhood interests and loyalties are inevitably giving way to adolescent ones.

Amy and Emily's scenario was familiar to me, an experienced sixth-grade teacher. I might have tolerated their behavior and their plight if I had not been challenged to help girls and struck by the similarity of their struggles with my own half-forgotten ones.

One morning before class I ambled over to Amy and her friends and asked, "What's going on with Emily?"

"I dunno."

"She doesn't sit with you guys anymore."

"So?"

"I notice something else too. You guys always turn your backs when she comes in, like you are telling secrets about her."

"Secrets? What do you mean? We're not telling secrets!"

"Well, you hold your hands up by your mouths. That says 'secrets' to me."

"So, we can say what we want. It's a free country."

"Yes, it is. But in this classroom, you can't hurt other people's feelings on purpose. You know I won't allow any kind of put-down in this class."

"You can't stop what we're saying quietly before class!"

"No, I can't. But I will ask you not to bring your hand up to your mouth in that 'I'm-telling-a-secret' way. Understood?"

"Yes, Ms. Strang."

It was a private conversation between the girls and me, not a public proclamation to the whole class. I had to remind them quite a few times, but holding my hand beside my mouth was usually enough. No secrets in this class became, over the years, a cornerstone of my expectations for all student behavior.

Of course a no-secrets rule was not enough to dissolve the

Emily-Amy feud. It was Amy, who seemed the tougher one, who led me to intervene more directly.

One day during break she ran into the room, sobbing. Years before, my instinct would have been to enfold and soothe her. Instead I asked calmly, "Hey, Amy. What's up?"

"She . . . she . . . told some kids that I . . . that I . . ."

"Wait, help me understand. Who is 'she'?"

"Emily!"

"How do you know she told them?"

"Andy said that Shelley told him that . . . I can't even *say* it, but she really hurt my feelings!"

"Hmmm. What does Emily say?"

"Emily?" Amy sniffs and looks directly at me. "Emily?"

"If you've been hearing rumors about what Emily said, you should ask Emily."

"Ask Emily? But Andy said—"

"I know Andy said Shelley said something. But if you really want to straighten this out, you should talk to Emily."

"Oh, I couldn't do that. She hates me."

"Would you like me to help? Why don't you get Emily to come here with you? I'll sit between the two of you on this bench . . ." Amy dashes away before I have any idea what I will do, sitting between them on that bench.

Ten minutes later they are back, both eager and reluctant. I pat the bench on either side. They sit and look at me, Amy still sniffing, Emily with shoulders hunched and arms crossed tight.

"Emily, hi. Amy tells me there are some rumors going around—"

Amy leaps in. "Yeah, Emily, how come you told Andy—"

"*I* told Andy? I didn't tell Andy anything. You are just jealous because—"

"Girls, girls, stay calm!".

"You really hurt my feelings."

"*I* hurt *your* feelings? How about *my* feelings?"

"Well, I didn't mean to, not really. It was just that Andy—"

"Andy doesn't matter."

"Hey, you're right. Do you remember the day we . . ."

I was invisible, unnecessary, and amazed at how little it took, really, to move these girls from playing he-said-she-said to talking directly to one another. They didn't become best friends again, but they did stop punishing each other, and many days in my classroom Amy and Emily sat happily together.

The future well-being of girls is too important for us to leave them alone. As teachers and parents, we cannot risk teaching them by our inaction that telling secrets, playing he-said-she-said, and stockpiling hurts are successful strategies for making and maintaining positive relationships. As a teacher and principal of many years, I have learned how not to leave them alone, how to push through their fierce resistance to adult intervention, how to move into a relationship with them where they may not listen to me, but they allow me to listen to their grievances and to initiate their listening to one another. Sometimes it works.

—Dorothy S. Strang, Illinois

Recognize When a Girl Needs Professional Help

Sometimes more dramatic action needs to be taken to keep both a girl and her peers safe.

TOUGH GIRL

My story starts when I was a little girl. I kept all of my emotions bottled up. I tried so hard to portray a "tough" image. Then in eighth grade I met a girl named Ashleigh, who was everything that I wanted to be and a little more. No one ever picked on her or called her names and got away with it. I became friends with her and started to imitate the way she lived life. I liked that she didn't take anything from anybody and that she was independent and not afraid to do anything.

When we were together, it seemed like everyone was afraid of us, and that made me feel good because I was so insecure about myself. When Ashleigh pierced her lip, it was a shock to the entire school. Then when she pierced mine, we started a trend. It was like that with everything we did. We never treated any other girls (except maybe one or two) with respect. In fact, we hardly treated *anyone* with respect.

One time me and a few other girls were playing basketball at recess and this girl took our ball, so I approached her and slapped her and got it back. The next few weeks Ashleigh and I would throw fish sticks at her during lunch because she smelled of fish.

Another time when we were at lunch, we were sitting next to an overweight girl. Ashleigh started making fun of her and calling her "beached whale." Then both of us started making fun of her. The next thing I knew one of our friends grabbed on to the overweight girl's fat and started jiggling it and laughing at her.

It hurts to think that I could be that cruel to another human being. I feel really stupid for all that I did. Some of the "jokes" we played on people actually affect the victims to this day.

—Anonymous

The author of this story goes on to relate how a confrontation with her mother, inspired by Ashleigh, led her into professional treatment. The help she received there made it possible for her to heal her relationship with her mom and to gain insight into her own actions.

Don't hesitate to get professional advice if a girl seems depressed and isolated. For the victim as well as the aggressor, involvement with RA can result in such negative psychosocial consequences as depression, loneliness, anxiety, peer rejection, acting-out behavior, and delinquency.

The effects of RA can show up differently in different girls. Some may develop disordered eating patterns as an attempt to deal with their unresolved negative feelings, while others may turn outward and direct their anger toward others. Regardless of *how* RA manifests itself, the message is clear: there is a *cost* for RA, and unfortunately for some, that cost has been much too high.

I grew up attending church regularly and developed a set of standards for myself: treating others as I wanted to be treated and not stealing, using the Lord's name in vain, gossiping, having premarital sex, or drinking alcohol, smoking, or doing drugs. I didn't care whether my friends or peers engaged in these activities, they just weren't right for me.

In freshman year of high school, I joined the highly regarded field hockey team, which consisted of intelligent, beautiful, athletic girls. I was homecoming princess and one of the most popular girls, all because I was on this state championship team. I started dating JT, the captain of the boy's soccer team, at the end of freshman year. He was popular, smooth, and well liked by the girls.

Sophomore year was not quite as exciting. Reflecting back, I now see times when my friends discovered my moral list to be uncool, childish, and an obstacle to having fun. Parties started taking place without me, and JT grew more and more impatient with my conviction not to have sex.

One day before class I sat flipping nonchalantly through JT's yearbook. Again and again, I read, "Remember the advice you told me about relationships, if you aren't happy . . . then get out!"

The phone rang around seven-fifteen that night. It was JT, calling much later than usual. "I don't think we should be together anymore," he blurted.

I crawled into my brand-new princess post bed and lay there

in a fetal position sobbing, feeling isolated and alone. I didn't even know why he broke up with me. When my mom heard what had happened, she wrapped her arms around me and rocked me back and forth. I finally cried myself to sleep in her arms.

A short time later I learned that JT had been cheating on me with my best friend for over a month. This was the beginning of my precious world falling apart. The pressure to conform grew more intense. The more I stood my ground, the more the world around me started to shatter.

I attended a sleepover where twenty-five girls crammed into a neatly finished basement to gossip. In the dark, on the hard floor, nasty comments and remarks were made about a friend of ours who wasn't able to attend. I lay there trying to determine what was the right thing to do. Stand up for her and stop the horrendous comments that filled the room, or continue on as if this was an acceptable way of treating your friends?

"I would appreciate it if you would please stop talking about Karen," I managed to blurt out. The room grew quiet and I could hear whispers from small groups all around me. Nothing more was said until they thought I was asleep. Then I became the victim of harsh gossip and nasty comments.

A few weeks later I entered the girls' bathroom, randomly opened a stall door, and read, "Julia Columbo is a suck-up, kiss-up bitch" written in black permanent marker. I wanted to die. How could people hate me so much?

Worse yet, I became forgotten. At the lunch table my

"friends" would talk about me as if I wasn't there. Invitations to sleepovers and remembrances of party episodes were exchanged in front of me.

High school is a challenging time for all adolescents. Sometimes both young men and women bottle their pain and emotions and carry them around like a shaken pop can waiting to explode. I didn't know how to stand up for myself for fear I would be considered a bitch. I wanted to be liked for the values and morals that set me apart, but instead I was judged. I wonder if people ever asked, "Who is Julia Columbo?"

—Julia Columbo, Michigan

CHANGE THE RA WAY OF LIFE

I don't even have a daughter yet, but I want to be part of something positive for girls so the world will be a different place if I do have one.

—YOUNG ATTORNEY, PREGNANT WITH HER
FIRST CHILD, ON VOLUNTEERING FOR THE
OPHELIA PROJECT

To truly make the world a better place for girls, the next generation of young women needs to learn to connect in positive ways with peers. By discovering their own inner strength and using it as a basis to both create a new culture and support others, girls can make RA a nonissue. This is easy to write about, but very hard to accomplish. In the words of one therapist, "It will take decades for our efforts now to pay off."

Discuss Alternatives

RA thrives because girls lack the courage or confidence to act in ways that end the dynamic and because they believe it is just a part of the adolescent experience to be endured. As adults we too often accept behaviors because we believe they are just part of growing up. Consider alternatives, and give a girl the self-esteem, confidence, and attitude of kindness that will give her strength to defuse an aggressor, support a victim, or mobilize bystanders. Ask girls, "What behaviors could substitute for aggressive or passive behaviors?" The following examples, all from girls who were asked to identify ways to end aggression, include giving compliments, changing the subject, being kind, switching to positive gossip, asking the aggressor to stop, focusing on internal attributes, and using affirmations.

Sometimes just raising a girl's awareness that she can change goes a long way toward rechanneling aggression, as seventeen-year-old Tanya discovered. Tanya, pretty and self-assured, crosses her legs in the lotus position and hugs her sweater around her as she talks. For the last eighteen months, she has been part of the Ophelia Sister Project in Warren, Pennsylvania. When asked what prompted her to take part in activities designed to help teenage girls deal with relational aggression and bullying, her expression changes.

"I was mean," she says, eyes suddenly dropping to focus on the floor. Regret is etched across her face as she reflects back on her behavior prior to becoming involved in the project. "I would start rumors about other girls, even my friends. A group of us almost made a game of it." It's hard to believe that a young woman who volunteers to teach middle school girls about forming healthy relationships with one another could ever have used such hurtful behavior, but her story is painfully familiar.

"Seventh grade was the absolute worst. I was in the guidance counselor's office every day for doing something mean. She would try and get me to talk to the other girls, to see their side of things. I would always be polite in her office, and for a while I would act nice, but then it would all start over again. You wouldn't believe how mean I was."

Tanya pauses, fidgeting with her hair, and obviously uneasy about remembering the way she used to be. Her blue eyes are pained as she continues her story.

"Then I got involved with Ophelia. The very first day of our training some older girls started talking about how girls are mean to each other, and they could have been describing me.

I was so uncomfortable sitting in that room, seeing my behaviors—or ones a lot like them—acted out. But the worst part was the next day, when one of the girls I tormented stood up and talked about how much people hurt her. She didn't accuse me in particular, but she was crying because she was so upset. That made *me* want to cry too. I was so ashamed I couldn't even look at anyone else."

Tanya's distress was still close to the surface, eighteen months later. However, since she joined a group of adult women and girls dedicated to ending relational aggression, her talking about other girls in a malicious way seems to be a thing of the past, along with her feelings of low self-esteem. She and her peers have learned a way to feel better about themselves and enjoy their relationships with other girls more. Confident kindness, rather than cruelty, is the guiding principle of their behavior.

"My friends still talk about other girls, but I just say *stop!*" Tanya concludes. "Most times they back down. If they don't, I actually stick up for the girl they are talking about, and then it usually stops. I just hope the girls I tormented have forgiven me; I know it's hard for me to forgive myself."

Girls themselves can often identify the best ways of changing perspectives, including the use of humor.

HARD FRIENDS

Last year I was really good friends with this one girl. She would write nasty notes and swear at me when we were mad, but then we would always patch up. This year things got kind of weird. First, her and her practically assistant made this singing/dancing group and kicked me out. Then they made up code names that ended with the word "gum" for people they hated, and mine was "Orange Gum!" At first I thought my friend was being mean because I was one of the fastest, strongest girls in my class and the other girl (who was new this year) was one of the fastest girls at her old school and thought she would be here too. Clue: They each promised to hate the person the other one did. Fact: That's not a good promise. Advice: When girls call you a bad name you never heard before, such as "tutor freak," say something like, "That is so creative! That's not on the list of bad names! How do you spell that? Is it two words or one?"

—M. L., age 10, Pennsylvania

Reward Kindness

Catch girls being kind and supportive of one another and compliment them on it. In the Cool to Be Kind Club, started by a concerned mother in Warren, Pennsylvania, acts of kindness are rewarded. Students are given pencils that say "I was caught being kind" when they do something positive for another. At home or in the classroom, a one-day activity for younger girls that introduces this concept is handing out poker chips for kind behaviors. At the end of the day, the person with the most chips gets special recognition and a small prize. Reinforcing positive behaviors, rather than focusing on negative ones, is a basic parenting practice most of us have used intuitively with our children as toddlers; it works with teens too. For older girls, high school awards that recognize community service, positive attitudes, and best motivators accomplish this same purpose.

Prevent Rumination

Help girls develop coping skills that do not involve others, such as listening to music, exercising, and keeping a journal. Dr. Nicole Werner, a developmental psychologist at

Washington State University, suggests that adolescent preoccupation with relationships can create a breeding ground for RA. When girls rehash peer conflicts over and over again with others, they may be more likely to retaliate with aggression. She suggests that parents can help girls curb this tendency by limiting telephone or computer time and substituting other activities.

Help Her Establish Relationship Boundaries

Sometimes the desire for friends leads a girl to forsake her own values in the quest for acceptance. While the question "If your friends jumped off a bridge, would you too?" often provokes rebellion, exploring what your girl *would* do in the name of friendship will give you both tremendous insight into her "relationship IQ."

This is important, because a girl who has no sense of self during adolescence can grow into a woman who continues to form unhealthy relationships throughout life. Identify specific behaviors that are unhealthy: allowing someone else to control your decisions; allowing someone to be verbally disrespectful to you, harass you, or threaten you. Help your girl determine where the line is that she will not cross, and reinforce her determination to stick to her principles.

BEST FRIENDS

Through my eyes, Lauren was my best friend. I loved her as much as a friend could ever love her best friend. We did everything together, and I told her everything.

The summer before ninth grade, Lauren invited me to go to the mall with her and a few other friends from school. I was so excited, I called off work and woke up early. She told me that she would call before she came to get me. Around noon I started to worry that she had never called. I thought she may have been running a little late, so I called her. To my surprise her father answered and notified me that she had already left for the mall.

I was so mad. When I confronted her, her response was, "You were never invited anyway."

Episodes like that happened all the time; to me that was just how Lauren was. After every little incident, I just shoved it in the back of my mind, thinking nothing of it. A few weeks into the school year, a very personal secret was being passed around my school, a secret that only my best friend would have known. I was so hurt to find out she was talking about me and also to know that this wasn't the first time. When I confronted her, her response was that she had never told anyone, but I knew she was lying. After that, I lost all respect for her.

I figured out that friends don't hurt each other. I never thought our friendship would end, especially like that.

—Sarah, age 15, Pennsylvania

Use Rituals of Respect

Ask girls, "How would it look for you to show respect to a friend, to yourself, to your teacher?" Ritual behavior can help girls develop respect, as happened at the Warren Dance Studio, where teacher Linda Dies implemented an opening and closing ceremony in which students bowed first to her, then to one another. The earlier these rituals are implemented, and the longer they remain part of the school, home, and community milieu, the more likely girls are to continue using them when on their own. For example, in many of the volunteer groups I work with, girls do not address adult women either as Miss or Mrs. Last Name or by their first names; instead they have a custom of calling all adult women by Ms. and then a first name. It's a simple but special act of courtesy that recognizes the bond between women of different ages.

Empower Girls to Problem-Solve

When given the encouragement to use their own creativity in problem solving and conflict resolution, girls can amaze you. Consider what happened when third- and fourth-grade teachers in Warren, Pennsylvania, asked the Ophelia Project for help in combating RA. Senior girls developed an intervention that involved role playing and reading *The Brand New Kid* by Katie Couric (Doubleday, 2000) to students. Not content to merely *respond* to problems, these impressive young women went on to place a "Dear Ophelia" suggestion box in the school cafeteria and are planning a play to raise awareness among their peers.

Help Girls Explore a New Way of Relating to Peers

This is especially crucial given the pressing developmental issues associated with identity during adolescence. As one high school volunteer in the Ophelia Project says, "The RA program really helped me figure out who I was and what was really important to me. Before that all I cared about was being accepted by other people. I didn't really take the time to figure out who I was or what I needed. I also found out that you're probably going to hurt other people if you are not happy with yourself."

"In eighth grade I got superdepressed," recalls a middle school girl. "I think that is when I quit caring about everything. I decided I wanted to be myself and I was tired of being fake. I couldn't stand it, I couldn't take it any longer. I was like, well, I will just be myself . . . and now I have even more friends."

When asked why some girls are *never* involved with RA, one middle school girl commented, "Because they know they are fine the way they are. They really don't find any reason to go make fun of someone or get into fights because they are just happy the way they are." If girls can find healthy ways to explore and become comfortable with who they are, they will be free to have positive, supportive relationships with one another.

Reframe Hurtful Behaviors

Certainly not every cruel behavior can or should be overlooked. However, young women who are secure in themselves are freed from the obsessive need to be liked by everyone. They also understand that aggression comes from a place of insecurity and fear; they can often "disarm" potential tormentors by not allowing their verbal arrows to hit a target. Some girls are naturally capable of such self-confident behavior, while others can learn to react confidently through preparing, processing, and practicing.

A mom whose daughter has been targeted might propose these questions, once the initial comforting has taken place: If this happens again, what might you do differently? What would have happened if you had ignored her? Can we walk through another situation and figure out how you could try to ignore aggression?

DEFLECTION

In my sophomore year of high school, I was dating a baseball/football player. We started going out right after he and my friend broke up. At first we didn't tell anyone, but when we did come out and tell people, boy, did the gossip start.

Some of my supposedly best friends were in on most of the gossip lines. It hurt me very badly. The very people I was turning to for advice were the ones starting the gossip.

My friendship with the ones who talked about me behind my back has never been the same. They broke the trust I had in them. For some of them it wasn't the first time they had broken my trust. In any relationship, whether it's a friendship or a girlfriend-boyfriend relationship, you need trust; once it has been broken, it's hard to regain.

When this all first happened, I thought that things were coming to an end. Like anything that happens in a teenager's life, it's dramatic. But I've overcome it and realized that it's all a part of growing up. We're not always going to have the same best friends. We have to learn to move on.

I thought that I was alone and wasn't going to have any friends after I quit talking to my former best friends, but I now have many new friends and two great best friends. Everyone should always know that no matter what the situation, you're never alone. There is always someone going through the same thing somewhere, somehow.

This situation taught me many things, but the greatest lesson was that you cannot let others get you down. Even if it is your best girlfriends, you have to ignore what they say about you and worry about yourself. All that matters is that you believe in yourself, know who you really are inside, and know that you can do anything, no matter what others say. We weren't put on this earth to judge others, just to live our lives the best we can.

Now I'm not worried about what everyone else thinks about me. There will always be people in your life who don't like you, especially other girls. It's a tendency we have. The bigger person is the one who ignores it and lets it slide, like I did and do now as well.

—Jennifer Schwoerer, age 17, Florida

Repeat, Repeat, Repeat

To truly change the way girls think, it isn't enough for moms to preach the message of confident kindness. Girls need to hear the same words from dads and other influential adults in their lives. Bulletin boards and theme activities in school can help remind them that it is far cooler to be kind than cruel. At home, never stop telling her that RA is wrong. You can even help her develop some affirmations that get this same idea across, which can be posted in places she frequents to help reinforce positive behaviors and boost self-esteem.

Change the Environment

As extreme as it may seem, sometimes the best option for dealing with prolonged RA is to make dramatic changes in the girl's environment, as shared in the following story.

MY STORY

People always say that beauty is on the inside, but I've yet to meet these people. My life is like many others in middle school, a living hell! And it's mostly girls that make my life miserable. It has nothing to do with who I am as a person; it has everything to do with the way I look.

When I was ten, my teeth grew in crooked. I went to an orthodontist who said that my jaw was too small for my teeth, so he would widen it and then put on braces. I went through all these treatments and had braces on and off before fifth grade was even over, but within a few months my teeth were crooked again. Obviously I got teased about this. The latest news from the orthodontist is that the final braces will go on next month.

My teeth aren't the only target. My eyebrows practically meet; I've been called unibrow and even owl. I started electrolysis last year but it's a long process. I've been harassed so many times because of my eyebrows, I thought I could rise above it.

In seventh grade I was redistricted to a new school and was looking forward to being with friends from elementary school, but the competition is unbelievable! I'm not talking about winning boyfriends either! Everything is about popularity. If you don't have it, showing up at school is almost like attempting suicide. Between classes I would always hang my head low so no one could tell it was me! And unlike elementary school, I don't have many friends in middle school, so life is tough.

I guess at times like this you turn to family for support, but my parents have been divorced since I was in kindergarten and my sister moved out a couple of years ago, so it's just me and my mom. During spring break I told her I wanted to be home-

schooled. Even though my mom wasn't sure about it, she supported me, changed her work hours, and agreed to it.

Basically I fled the scene so I wouldn't be depressed anymore. While I wouldn't recommend running away like this (I
really wish I had been able to cope with school), things have
begun to turn around for me. Even my family has admitted this
was the right decision.

To all the girls out there with the same problem, don't run
away. Do whatever you have to do before you decide to leave.
In middle school life can be rough, especially when other girls
turn on you! They brag, tease, and bully you for different reasons. It's one of the toughest things you'll ever have to deal
with in school—maybe even in life.

—Justine, middle schooler, Florida

This young lady's story is made all the more poignant by
the stunning black-and-white picture of herself she enclosed
with her story, depicting an attractive girl with a well-
proportioned jaw and perfect eyebrows.

Here's another story about the drastic measures a mother
took to remove her daughter from an ongoing RA drama.

GIRLS HURTING GIRLS: OUR PERSONAL
EXPERIENCE

Although I am a clinical psychologist with a private practice
and have worked with other girls who were victims of aggression, when my own daughter reached this age, it was hard to
see at first. Because she has a learning disability that made

dealing with the school difficult, I was so busy focusing on educational issues, I missed the torture she was going through socially, and she was unable to describe it to me.

What happened to her? She was quite uniquely beautiful, being a nice blend of races, and in ninth grade was one of three freshman girls invited to the senior prom. She got taller and more beautiful as the years went on and eventually modeled a bit as well. This made the local girls extremely jealous. People were constantly seeing her in magazines on the shelves of the drugstore. The boys loved her; the girls hated her. However, the girls used her when they could, because wherever Nicole was, the boys were.

Although she was not sexually promiscuous, word was spread that she was a "slut." She hated life, became suicidal, and made two attempts to kill herself. She was crying for help, and no one understood what was happening, not even me.

In the year after high school the ramifications continued to be a problem for her because we live in a rural community several hours from the nearest big city. I suggested she move to a nice city in the southern end of the state, gave her a small bankroll and a car, and helped her move myself. She has been home twice since and has found that she no longer cares what these people think of her and wants nothing to do with them. More importantly, her sense of self-esteem is much higher than it was when she lived here and was a victim of the aggression.

—Dr. Patricia Ferguson, California

Discuss Unconditional Positive Acceptance and Forgiveness

Girls who feel confident about themselves can approach others with the same attitude. Expressing acceptance and being able to forgive a hurt are two ways a girl can use her personal strength to defuse RA.

OUT OF THE IN CROWD

"Kristin, can I have a tissue?" I remember the way his sneering smile asked the question.

"What? Why would I have a tissue?" I stared back, trying to make sense of the words just asked. Before I fully understood exactly what was happening, I heard laughter erupt from behind me. I turned to see the faces of two of the most popular girls in the seventh grade, girls whom I wished to be, look, and act like, girls who I had always wished would pay attention to me, befriend me, or make me one of their own.

The words spread: "Kristin stuffs her bra, that's why her boobs look so much bigger this year." "I heard she uses a whole box of tissues every morning." "What a loser! There are other ways to get guys to look at you."

I couldn't believe what I was hearing. It was true my chest had inflated considerably over the summer, two whole sizes to be exact, but not from a box of Kleenexes. Instead it was that normal thing called growing up, or perhaps, as my mother had so delicately put it, that summer I had "blossomed." I spent the rest of the day shuffling through the halls with my head down to avoid the stares and comments whispered just loud enough for me to hear as I walked past.

Returning home, I ran to the one person who was always there to make me feel beautiful—my mother. She held me and let me cry, telling me that I was perfect and what did I care what they thought anyway. But that was exactly the problem—I did care. I wanted everyone to think I was beautiful. I wanted to be accepted for who I was and what I looked like. I wanted to be just like those girls who had laughed at me.

I never knew exactly why they started that rumor about me. Perhaps they really thought I did stuff my bra; perhaps they were jealous that I was one of the few girls who actually needed the bra they were wearing; perhaps I was just another target in their own search for self-discovery. Whatever the reason, they had brought me down. Years later I asked one of the girls about it. Her head hung as she remembered her awful words and listened to my account of that day.

I hope my experiences and stories will help other girls realize the effects of their actions as well as make many of the victims realize they are not alone. Perhaps my influence can play a small role in putting an end to girls hurting each other. It's a good thing I was never exactly accepted by the in crowd. I would not be the strong, independent woman that I am today if I had been.

—Kristin Blake, age 17, Pennsylvania

Talk About the Role of Boys in Girl-Girl Conflict

Girls learn early on to value relationships with boys over relationships with girls. Too often aggression between girls occurs because of a boy, as recognized by this senior girl who works as a mentor with middle school girls: "We do try to tell them to limit the topic, not to talk about boys as much. Because sometimes they ramble on about the boys so, we are kind of trying to shy away from that. . . . But some of the situations do involve guys, like, 'I am going out with Bob and my best friend Sally really likes Bob, and Sally is saying that I cheated on Bob and Bob got mad at me,' and stuff like that."

A classic example is the girl who goes out with her best friend's boyfriend, either before or after the best friend and boyfriend have broken up. Long after the young man has gone his merry way, the girls who were formerly friends continue to dislike and aggress against each other. As one of the counselors at Camp Ophelia quizzed during a role play of this scenario, "What's wrong with this picture?"

Encourage girls to think about the dynamics of friendship when a romance is involved. Separate out who is responsible for what: Should a girl alone be blamed for going out with a friend's boyfriend, or are both equally culpable? How should a girl handle situations where a friend's boyfriend flirts with her or asks her out? When does a romantic interest override a friendship? What is the best way to share information about a budding romance with a friend, when she has formerly been involved with the same boy?

Jess, a senior high school student who participated in the Warren Ophelia Sister Project, describes how conflict over a boy divided not just two girls but her whole crowd of friends: "There were about ten of us girls who used to get together once a week for a girls' night out. Then two of the girls got into a fight over a boy, and pretty soon everybody was taking sides, and our whole group was divided. We stopped doing things together like we used to, which really upset me. I went to both of the girls and tried to reason with them.

"I told them, 'You don't have to be best friends to be polite to each other,' because the tension between them was splitting us apart. Before Ophelia, I might have felt compelled to choose sides too, but now I know talking things out and solving the conflict are better choices."

While the relationship between her friends is still tense, Jess has hopes they will be able to patch things up soon. Best of all, she's not caught up in the dilemma of siding with one group over the other, as she might have been previously.

"I talk to everyone, even though in my mind I do sort of see one girl as more right than the other," she says. "It doesn't help anyone for our friendships to be divided over a fight about a boy."

Strategies 8–10:
PROVIDE SUPPORT
OFFER HER OTHER OUTLETS AND OPPORTUNITIES

It actually can be very inspiring. You want to take action to make a difference.

—A YOUNG WOMAN WHOSE HIGH SCHOOL
EXPERIENCE WAS MARRED BY RA

Girls who are caught up in RA dramas often fail to see alternative ways in which their energy could be used. Several times we've heard from aggressors and bystanders that RA was just something to do, a behavior motivated by boredom and perpetuated by a lack of guidance and alternatives. For victims, empowerment often leads to social activism and a desire to show others that they do have options and can free themselves from the target role.

Create and Relate Around RA

Girls need to get the message out to other girls. Often, expressing oneself through art is not only a powerful therapy, it builds confidence. Creating something tangible to capture a painful or joyful emotion improves mental health for reasons not fully understood; it helps girls connect with one another in ways that transcend everyday social interactions. A play, painting, song, or story seems to get feelings expressed in a positive way, and studies suggest that adolescents in particular respond better to art than to other forms of therapy.

Promote Positive Emotional Expression

The goal of confident kindness is not to create a cohort of girls who are self-effacing and eager to please because of an inner sense of insecurity. By learning to recognize genuine feelings and understand what to do with them, girls achieve a sense of internal safety and well-being that permits them to approach others with an attitude of kindness.

"I encourage girls to journal a lot," says one guidance counselor in a middle school. "That helps provide some baseline where they can look back a month ago and see how they were feeling then, compared to now."

Journals also offer an opportunity for girls to gain insight by looking beneath the words at the emotion that precipitated them. Adults and mentors can also offer a constructive outlet for emotional expression simply by making sure to ask a girl about her day, about what happened that was good or bad.

If your girl is artistic, encourage her to create a collage of positive and negative images from the media of girls interacting, and post it someplace prominent so others can see it and comment (home, school, a community building, church, synagogue, or religious education institution—anywhere girls and adults can see and discuss it). She might create her own website for this purpose or design notecards, book covers, and other visual art that moves the focus away from competition and conveys affirmative images of adolescent girls. Workshops on filmmaking, visual art, or graphic design can help her experiment with different modalities and techniques that give her further control over media messages.

The Ophelia Project worked with a midwestern suburban school to empower girls as spokespersons against RA. Through small group work facilitated by older mentors, girls created collages, posters, and plays to convey the message that

RA hurts everyone involved. The most memorable event was a "talk show" complete with a hostess and "experts," with guest appearances from aggressors, victims, and bystanders. Those girls not actually involved on the stage were audience participants who provided questions and feedback that made the show much like those on television.

The poem that follows is one girl's creative response to RA.

The whispers in throats are knives in the back, stabbing innocent lives with untruths.

The lies that are screeched, are blows to the head, knocking the air out of souls.

The taunts that are roared, are swift slaps to the face, stinging and burning the heart.

The pressure is bombs, going off one-by-one, blowing you slowly to bits.

The anger is eggs, growing larger and larger, until they are forced to burst.

The jealousy is a disease, scattering among all, attacking consecutive souls.

The peace is a sun, slowly setting, but we know it must once again rise.

—Morgan Smith, seventh grade, North Carolina

Start an Anti-RA Campaign

Girls need to be reminded of how to act and what is expected of them. This is a given in elementary school, where creative bulletin boards and classroom rules are posted on the walls so everyone can see them. When children go to middle school, the bulletin boards disappear, and very few, if any, teachers spend time going over rules for behavior. No one is totally clear about what is expected, and so limits are tested. This puts adults in a reactive rather than proactive role, responding to trouble and disruptions as they emerge.

If we want our children to follow a code of conduct that celebrates inclusive caring and kindness, then we need to remind them of the rules on a consistent basis. Tell girls, "Here's what I expect. Here are the behaviors that correspond to inclusive caring." Spell them out. Similarly, "Here are behaviors that will not be tolerated: eye rolling, rumor spreading, intentionally hurting others' feelings, leaving someone out," and so on. The first step to changing behavior is to be mindful of it, so infiltrate your girl's world with positive messages about how to treat people. Encourage her and her friends to adopt a zero tolerance policy toward RA.

"I think the victim needs to confront the aggressor or aggressors and say, You hurt my feelings and I didn't appreciate it and if you don't want to hang out with me, that's fine, I will go hang out with somebody else," a sixteen-year-old Ophelia Sister Project member suggests. "I think if the victim does that, then the aggressor or aggressors will realize, oh my gosh, and be really surprised and think, Oh well, she doesn't want to hang out with us. She is going to go hang out with somebody else; maybe I am missing out on something. So make them think twice about how they interacted with you."

With your support, have girls approach influential administrators, teachers, coaches, and others and suggest that the school adopt a slogan such as "Help, Don't Hurt." Grab some artistic types who like to have their work featured in the paper and commission their help in creating banners, flags, and posters. Make sure they get lots of press for their hard work! (Most kids love to get their picture in the paper.)

Create a safe place and safe activities for girls. Offer to start a club where girls can work on building healthy rather than hurtful relationships. Some good models are Club Ophelia, GENAustin, the Girls Club of America, the Girl Scouts of America, the Ophelia Project, and many local efforts at high schools, such as the one profiled later. Each focuses on gathering girls together to create an environment where issues related to RA can be explored and resolved with help and supervision from adults and mentors.

Lobby for an official "Safe Place for Kids" at school or a "Cool to Be Kind" day. The place can be any physical location where kids can go to feel secure, a sort of grown-up time-out area. Ideally, of course, *every* place should be a safe place for kids, but the symbolism of a room or area designated as such and decorated by kids themselves has special meaning. An annual Cool to Be Kind day, when students accumulate stickers or poker chips for kind behaviors observed by adults, can be an event that sets permanent change in motion. This kind of activity requires minimal expense and can be coordinated by a teacher or any concerned adult. Families can even institute their own versions of Cool to Be Kind days.

Initiate an effort that will require everyone to make a small personal commitment. This might mean signing a contract to intentionally include others for one week. Schoolwide or community projects work particularly well if older girls spearhead the effort to get buy-in from younger students. For example, middle school girls could organize an "Everybody In" day for elementary school students to promote including others. Once girls are put in the position of role-modeling for others, the pressure to continue kind behaviors after the lesson plan is put away can be a great motivator.

Encourage Her to Volunteer

Important strategies for helping girls cope with RA are distraction, esteem building, and reframing. Connecting her with others, changing her perspective, and building confidence are ways to accomplish these outcomes, and volunteer work is a way to combine all three. Helping others shifts a girl's focus from internal to external, giving her a sense of accomplishment and temporarily or permanently changing her outlook in a way that provides an antidote for bruised feelings. Dr. Nicole Werner encourages parents to help girls develop competencies that are not directly tied to friendships, so that these competencies can act as protective factors throughout life.

Have your girl pick something that interests her, such as working with animals or small children, and make the needed connections. For girls who are part of a group that seems perpetually caught up in RA dramas, community service is a great way to channel their energy into something positive and to ground their relationships in a shared sense of compassion and caring for others.

Provide Opportunities for Genuine Success

Sometimes smaller changes that give a girl the chance to succeed can go a long way toward improving her self-esteem, which then makes her a more attractive friend to others. New opportunities and new friends have a way of offsetting the hurt of RA, even if a girl might never seek them out for herself, as in the following stories.

TRUE SUCCESS

In the small school that I went to, during the final week the eighth graders spent all of their time practicing for the grand pomp and circumstance of the coming graduation. Halfway through that week, during one of our infrequent breaks, my "friends" asked me to come over to where they had made a semicircle in one corner of the hall.

Naturally I went over to talk with them. They rather calmly but pseudo-sadly informed me that I was just too immature to be friends with them anymore. I was crushed, but I couldn't run away, crying, to nurse my wounded ego alone. Oh no. Our break was over and I had to resume my place in our stuffy practice.

Everyone around me wanted to know what was wrong, because I was doing a poor job of holding back tears. Of course I couldn't tell them; I was too humiliated by what "they" had said.

That day for lunch one of the girls had her mother bring pizza for us. I stormed off in the general vicinity of our local ministore, saying something about getting my own food. Halfway there I stopped in a nice secluded place and cried all through our lunch break.

That night I was buried in my bed considering a future as a hermit when my mom came in. She asked if I was okay. I burst into tears and ended up telling her everything that had happened. She held me as I cried myself out.

I thought for a long time that this incident would scar me for the rest of my life, but that summer I was privileged to be accepted to the 4-H California Focus trip in Sacramento. I was frightened because I didn't know anyone there, and my recent experience had led me to believe that I would never be able to make friends again. To my utter amazement, as soon as I arrived, I started making friends.

I am now a junior in high school. I realize no one is ever happy trying to be popular. I gave up all the nonsense of popular clothing and makeup, because I know that that is not who I really am.

If I had not been put through such a harrowing experience,

I would never have come to such a conclusion and would not be the person I am today. And that would have been a pity, because I find myself to be more satisfactory and more natural than I have ever been.

—Ambria Renner-Cox, age 17, California

USED TO

I love school. I love reading and writing, science and social studies. I love talking with friends at lunch and playing with them at recess. I love it all. Wait a minute. *I used to love it all.*

Jane and I met at the end of fourth grade. By the time fifth grade started, we were probably the happiest pair of friends imaginable. Then Laura, a popular girl, started being friendly to Jane. Laura is cute and perky, but she also talks behind girls' backs and is mean and pouts if she doesn't get her way.

I was worried about Jane's new friendship with Laura, but I didn't want to say much. Each day that I kept my feelings in made me hurt worse. If Jane and Laura were together and I was nearby, they would look at me, whisper, and giggle. When I asked what they were saying, all they would say was "Nothing."

My only sanctuary was my mom. I would go home and cry and tell her about my horrible day. One afternoon she asked me, "What are some of the things that make you most angry about the way Jane is treating you?"

I told her that whenever we were together and alone outside of school, we would have a lot of fun, but whenever I said hi to her in school, she and Laura would exchange glances and Jane would look past me like she was embarrassed about our friendship. When I tried to talk to Jane about what was happening, she would say, "It's not like that," or, "You need to lighten up." One of the worst experiences I ever had was when we were at our other friend's house. We were playing duck, duck, goose and Jane was it. She tapped me on the head and said, "Ugly duck."

My mom and dad helped me see that no matter what Jane said, she wasn't behaving as a true friend would. One day I told Jane that I didn't like her anymore and that our friendship was over.

My mom has suggested that this summer I invite girls on my softball and soccer teams to do things. In the fall I plan to hang out and play with lots of different people and not to depend on one best friend. That would be my advice to anyone else being bullied. Oftentimes, the person you thought would always be your friend, well, changes.

—C. M., age 10

GIVE HER A DOSE OF EMOTION LOTION TO SOOTHE AND SUPPORT

That's what moms do—one hug and she can make you forget, at least for a little bit, how bad you feel.
—THIRTEEN-YEAR-OLD GIRL WHO WAS A
  BYSTANDER WHEN HER BEST FRIEND WAS
  VICTIMIZED BY RA

Whether a girl is victim, bystander, or aggressor, she feels isolated and alone, sure that no one else is like her or can appreciate the unique obstacles she faces, be they bad skin, excess weight, flat chest, or big nose. To provide her with the emotional support she needs, concerned adults need to address both her low self-esteem and her sense of being unlike—or different from—others.

She Is Not Alone

Using role plays, storytelling, reading, or videos to promote insight into how another girl feels (and how her feelings are similar to your own girl's) can be a powerful tool. The stories in this chapter are representative of dozens if not hundreds of others we have received.

Girl Wars

We were going to spend the last day of sixth grade at an amusement park. The teachers told us to pick groups. From my point of view that was not the best decision, but it was great to know that they thought we were mature enough to handle this on our own.

One day during break Amy asked me if she could be in my group. I replied that it was great with me as long as it was okay with the rest of my group. After I found out that some other girls did not want that, I was confused. I did not know how to tell Amy, or if I was the right person to do it, especially since I would not be speaking from my heart. I tried to dodge this obstacle by ignoring it.

This worked until I observed her crying in a corner at lunch. My throat tightened. My group got together and we all invited her in.

Now that I am much friendlier with her, I think my other friends and I were not paying enough attention to her to look deeper inside of her and find that she is actually a very sweet girl. Amy never stopped the group from having a fabulous time. I cannot understand why we had to make such a big deal over such a minor addition while hurting her feelings.

Although this was a terrible thing to do, I have learned a lot. I hope that other girls can learn from my faults instead of making them.

—Lauren Kahn, seventh grade, North Carolina

Girls in middle school are often so desperate to be part of a group, they will stay in it even when mistreated. "I was a victim in fifth and sixth grade like you won't believe," recalls one high school student. "I know what it is like. You are so alone, but you go to the people who pick on you because they know that you are alive. As if they are the only ones who really know that you are there. I needed the connection no matter how bad it was for me. It was better to be alone and be with people than just to be alone."

In their longing for a friend, no matter what the personal costs, girls can move between the roles of victim, aggressor, and bystander. Recent research underscores the fluid relationship between the aggressor and the victim; i.e., one day "Sue" is the bully, the next, she is a victim.

GIRLS HURT GIRLS

I started high school with a set of new people who were all strangers, except for Natalie and Claire, who were my closest friends at the time and not good ones at that. Natalie was the controller: she would decide who she wanted to be best friends with for a few days and then change her mind, constantly swapping between Claire and myself.

When I was chosen to sit next to Natalie, I did feel a twinge of guilt knowing Claire was being left out, but I didn't dare speak out in case it would be me who was left out next. When that happened, it was awful. It hurt so much to have to sit behind them and listen to their whispers and giggles. Soon I started to realize that I was obviously less desirable than Claire.

So the search began. I had to start by becoming friends with a different group of girls so I could hopefully forge a relation-ship with one of them as a best friend. I don't know where my need or desire to have one best friend came from, yet it was something that I just had to achieve.

Looking back, I do not understand why Claire or I put up with Natalie, yet we did. We each tried our hardest to win over the affections of Natalie so we would be the favorite of the week and not have to sit alone in classes. So before I had even finished my first year at high school, I experienced how other girls could hurt me.

—Shelly Baker, age 20, United Kingdom

Other girls have found themselves in similar situations, one minute a victim, the next a bystander or even aggressor. Often the role switch is not even a conscious decision but occurs before a girl realizes what has happened; she cannot then "take back" the behavior.

WORDS HURT

While many people consider high school a prime time for friends and socializing, the case has always been different for me. I am well aware of the impact of girls hurting girls; I wit-ness this cruelty nearly every day and have been a victim myself.

For some reason, girls also love to gossip. I'll admit, it is often hard to refrain from this terrible habit, but it is very hurtful. For example, two of my friends are very close to another girl, whom they spend a lot of time with and talk to constantly. However, as soon as she steps away, they immediately begin talking about her nastily. When I listen to them talk like this, it makes me wonder—what do they say about me when I'm not around?

Recently I told one of my friends a funny story that involved my best friend and me. However, my friend manipulated the story around and told my best friend that I was talking about her and saying mean things. Of course this was not true, but I was told that my friend in turn said rude things about me. My best friend and I did not speak for a few days. When we finally put aside our differences and talked, we discovered that everything we had been told that the other said was a big lie.

This year I became friends with a girl that all of my fellow friends are also close to. We got along really well, and I was happy with the friendship. However, when her birthday arrived, she decided to have a party—and invited every single one of our friends but me. To make matters worse, she would gush about the upcoming party in front of me and try to rub it in my face. The day after the party, I talked to my best friend on the phone, and she immediately brought up the dreaded topic. "The party was awesome! Everyone was there!" she squealed. This hurt. Not everyone was there; I wasn't there.

I am a naturally shy person, which has created many difficulties. Sometimes girls will think that I am purposely ignoring them, which is not the case at all.

Although it hurts that others don't take the time to truly get to know me, I know that it is their loss. When it comes right down to it, what others say is not important; it's what's in your heart that counts. And remember, those who stand by you and don't listen to what others say are your true friends—and that's the most important thing of all.

—Angela Haupt, age 15, Pennsylvania

At every venue when stories like these are being shared, there is absolute silence in the room. A moment after the words end, nearly every girl or mother in attendance affirms the reality of the stories and the personal impact on their lives. Nothing seems to open the hearts of women of all ages as much as discussions about friendships turned sour.

If you are interested in developing this kind of forum using prepackaged materials, check Appendix B for more information on a booklet titled *Wary Mary or Savvy Sue, Which Are You? A Primer of RA Facts for Girls*, which comes with a discussion guide.

Emphasize Her Strengths

A natural tendency is for victims in particular to blame themselves or feel they deserve the aggression they receive from another girl. When you identify and compliment her on her strengths, rather than belittling her for responding inappropriately or feeling overwhelmed by the hurt, you give her important support. Following is one mother's commentary on how confidence and a belief in oneself help a girl during difficult times.

SOCIAL WORK

I am a social worker and mother of a ninth grader who attends a middle school where seventh, eighth, and ninth grades are together. I feel so strongly about the behavior that is being demonstrated by young girls that I am running for the school board.

At my daughter Ann's school, every day a few boys would come over to the lunch table where she and her friends sat and call the girls "whores" and "bitches." Finally Ann asked this boy to stop calling her friends such names. He verbally attacked my daughter, calling her a "bitch" and a "whore," and said she was "too f—— ugly to f——." It shocked my daughter, and she walked away but was crying.

When she told me, I felt it was past the point of letting the "kids work it out"! I went to the school and had a talk with the principal, very aware that I, as a fifty-year-old woman, do not have to put up with such language at my worksite.

The principal called in the young man and my daughter as well as another girl (who verified the abuse). The boy apologized of course and did do better. The kicker was that this friend of my daughter's called her later and told her "never to get her involved in anything like this again." Again, my daughter was shocked and told her she didn't think they should be friends anymore.

I then called an adult friend of mine, who boldly told me that my daughter was "out of line" and that kids don't want another kid acting like a mom and telling them what they can do and not do. This adult then went on to say that my daughter would be shunned by the other girls for speaking up, and they did shun her, but I think at this mother's urging!

I felt bad for my daughter, but she has so many social worker skills in her that she chose to go sit at another table. She had enough self-confidence to feel good about standing up for her friends. Ironically, the girl who said she didn't want to be involved later started sitting at Ann's lunch table and admitted that the boy was verbally harassing her and she had been too scared to do anything.

I am proud of my daughter but ashamed of the other girls and the mother who condoned this type of behavior.

—Rebecca Baker, Kentucky

Another aspect of confidence is believing you can make a difference. As part of her training activities to help girls identify ways they respond to RA, Ophelia Project executive director Mary Baird uses creative activities that make the same point: it only takes one girl to change the dynamic.

She says, "Sometimes I use a story that a high school girl has written about how one single girl can make a significant difference. Another thing I do is bring in a pair of big shoes and have each girl stand in them to get an understanding of how others feel. I literally put them in the 'victim's' shoes or the 'girl in the middle's' shoes or the 'aggressor's' shoes. There are a number of ways to help them try to get into the roles others play and to identify ways to make things different."

Share Your Stories

Believe it or not, girls like to hear stories about their parents as children. Although they may not view them as credible gauges of what to do in the current culture, they still want to know that "once upon a time," mothers, aunts, and other female relatives faced problems similar to their own. More than one girl has been encouraged or comforted by a story about a friendship struggle their own mother went through, which helps them realize that it's not true that they're alone or that "No one else could possibly understand how I feel."

A middle school guidance counselor observes, "Moms are so close to this stuff. Sometimes their own issues from the past surface again when their daughters go through tough times." The following stories show how sensitivity to past hurts can prompt mothers to intervene in the lives of girls and help them learn from their parents' experiences.

THE CALL

I was just starting my junior year in a new high school and hadn't made any friends. During a visit to my brother's house, a call came for me.

Taking the receiver, I answered nervously, "Hello?"

There was no warning, no hesitation, just an unmistakably angry female voice yelling, "*B**ch!*" followed by a click. I stood there for a moment, phone in hand, trying to fight the lump forming in my throat. I didn't want to cry in front of everyone, so I masked the look of shock on my face and hung up the phone with a shrug.

"Wrong number," I explained. Inside I felt like I'd been punched in the stomach.

The first few weeks in my new school had been rough, and the feeling that I now had a nameless enemy to worry about made going back almost unbearable. It was a small town where everyone seemed to know everyone else, and I was very shy. I found myself looking up, down, anywhere but into their faces—hoping to avoid the one behind the phone call that haunted me. It could have been any one of them.

Fortunately, several weeks later, a really nice guy came up to me at my locker and began a conversation that ended in an invitation to a homecoming party. I was so happy to have someone show an interest in me that I jumped at the chance to go out. Eventually I made a small circle of friends and told myself it didn't matter if some unknown person still hated me for whatever reason.

I never did find out who made that phone call, but I never forgot it or the pain it inflicted. What may have been only a moment of frustration for the caller was an ongoing assault to my wavering self-confidence. Words can be the most powerful weapon.

Recently my daughter and a friend were talking about some kids at school. The conversation, as usual, turned to boys.

"Oh, he is so hot! I'm so bummed that he likes that new girl."

"Yeah, I can't believe he likes her," said my daughter. "She's such a snob."

Considering my past, I couldn't help adding my two cents.

"You know," I casually suggested, "appearances really can be deceiving. Maybe she's just shy." I ignored their doubtful looks and continued. "I'll never forget when I was the new girl in school. I was at my brother's house one day after school and the phone rang . . ."

—Heather M. Haapoja, Minnesota

CROSSED

When I heard my then eight-year-old daughter Sofie's friend ask her, "Who do you like better, me or Hannah?" I was livid. Driven by the memory of a similar question asked of me many years earlier, I burst into the room and, trying to keep my voice somewhat even, announced, "That's a question that should never be asked!"

Sofie and her friend looked up at me with a combination of surprise at my outburst and annoyance at my intrusion, but the question went unanswered.

When I was eight, I had a friend named Mary. She was a thin, pale girl with thick brown hair chopped off at her chin, and though she wore pretty dresses with puffy skirts and bows in the back, she was rather plain.

Later that year I became friends with Monique, who had straight blond hair and freckles—far superior, I felt, to my short brown curls. Her long, agile limbs contrasted sharply with my shorter, stockier ones. I was flattered that she seemed to enjoy my company.

Predictably, Monique and Mary didn't like each other, and for much of that spring, I yo-yoed between them. I wanted them to be friends, I wanted us all to get along, but in reality, they were too different.

My having two best friends must have bothered Monique. One day, at the end of recess, all three of us were standing together, and she grabbed the opportunity.

Provide Support

153

"Who's your real best friend, me or her?" she asked, her eyes catching mine and darting momentarily in the direction of Mary. She was directly in front of me, while Mary was between us on my left.

I'm sure Mary was as unprepared for the question as I was; it was not the kind of thing she dwelled on. I felt caught, trapped in a moment I hadn't asked for but felt compelled to resolve. My mind raced, juggled, toyed with diplomacy as the seconds passed.

"I can't answer that!" I should have declared, or laughed it off with "What a silly question!" Instead I tried to have it all. I held Monique's eyes as I said, "You are," while my left hand moved slowly over toward Mary, two fingers crossed.

"You see? I don't mean it," I vainly attempted to telegraph to Mary, focusing on my fingers, trying to get her to look. "It means it's a lie."

I don't know if she ever looked down to notice my hand; I don't know if she even heard my reply to Monique. She never said a word to me about it, then or later. In an instant, the bell rang and we were herded inside.

That pretty much ended my friendship with Mary. We weren't in the same class in fourth grade, and I moved on easily. When Monique and her family relocated at the end of the summer, I barely noticed.

Until I had children of my own, I never realized I didn't have to answer Monique's question that day. Instead I came up with the best solution I could, a fiasco, it turned out, and the moment is seared in my memory. I crossed two fingers, but really I crossed two friends.

—Susan Hodara, New York

Have Older Girls Share Their Wisdom

While adults can help girls by recalling RA situations they dealt with, the best source of support may come from other girls who are a year or two older. These girls can still remember the hurt of being an aggressor, bystander, or victim quite clearly, but they often have the insight to provide concrete solutions that can work.

As she looks back, a graduate student recalls her experiences as painful at the time, but ones she is ultimately thankful for:

> I think with me it kind of started in high school. In junior high I was like one of the popular people, but in ninth grade I started to really notice that everybody would go out and drink. I would not do that, and the guys stopped asking me out because they knew I wouldn't do that and I wouldn't go to parties. And I was still a part of the popular girls, but they started doing things behind my back. There were parties that they didn't invite me to; my mother would ask me why I didn't go to the parties, and I would tell her they didn't invite me. It was actually a really tough time for me because I wanted to be a popular girl. By tenth grade people were inviting me less and less, and guys wouldn't ask me out. I just couldn't take it anymore. I was so upset, I couldn't do the right thing, and all I was getting was crap from everybody for it. My parents couldn't understand; I tried to tell them, but they were friends with the other girls' parents.
>
> Whenever I had a party, I had to invite everyone. There was no student whom I could not invite. I got excluded from things, but I had to invite them to my party. I would say to

my mom this isn't fair, they didn't invite me, I am not inviting them. She said that's not how things go.

When girls talked about each other behind their backs, it
was hard not to join in, but I figured if this is what I am going
to do, I have to be consistent. I find that a lot of girls have a
hard time because they want not to gossip and sometimes
they don't, but sometimes they do and that's almost worse
than just doing it all the time.

There were girls who wrote nasty notes to me and I didn't
even know why, but I guess they couldn't figure out why I
wouldn't do what they did. They couldn't figure out why I
wouldn't talk about people.

Although she is now grateful that her mother pushed her to
be different from her friends, at the time it was painful to go
through rejection.

HINDSIGHT

Two years ago I had two best friends that I always went out
with on the weekends or called nonstop on the telephone. (I
guess it's a teen phase.) Anyway, it became a routine, or tradi-
tion, among the three of us, until one of us started to stray
from the group. At first it was cool; she was meeting new people and hanging out with them occasionally. However, over
time she stopped calling or wanting to do things on the weekends. It's really hard to watch your "best friend" ignore you or
stop calling. When this happens, it feels a little like betrayal.

Every time we confronted our former "best friend" about
the issue, she would deny doing anything wrong. Soon we were
no longer friends, and no longer talking. The good old silent
treatment—it's a classic with teens.

What happened next surprised me a bit. Her new group of friends turned on her. They cornered her late one night and threw words back and forth. The next day, she had absolutely no friends.

A teen's biggest fear is being alone, in my opinion. It's hard to go to school and have to sit alone in the cafeteria or in class, but she did it. Not because she wanted to, but because she hadn't kept more friends than just those few.

My friend today still holds a grudge, because she knows we talked about her behind her back. She also did the same to us, but it doesn't matter to me. I tried to talk to her many times, but she shut me out. Our friendship is still not the same, but at least I don't have to leave high school with hatred toward her or with her hating me.

The end lesson here is, never assume you'll be best friends forever. You will have fights. Stay alert, and when you do get in fights, it's important not to hold grudges. Someday you may want to rekindle the relationship, or even just set the record straight by saying sorry. Over time the feeling of hate will leave you, no matter what role you played in the friendship.

After high school you will be alone if you go on to university. It's a fresh start, and you'll have to make friends all over again. It's important to realize how you handled friendships in the past, so you can learn from them for the future.

—Leanne R. DeLong, age 18, Canada

The insights of Jen, which follow, illustrate how one girl can give advice to others on lessons learned the hard way.

IF ONLY I COULD DO IT OVER

Dee was one of those girls who sat alone and read thick novels during lunch and asked questions about the space-time continuum during history. The preppy, popular people wanted nothing to do with her, so of course we became fast friends. She had one other friend, Tina, who was in some of my classes. The three of us got along quite well, and for a while things were great. We had people to sit with at lunch, friends to talk to on the phone at night, and group projects that worked out great.

But, as they say, three's a crowd. Tina was a diehard *X-Files* enthusiast and eventually she hooked me on it too. Dee's parents wouldn't allow her to watch it, so she was more and more left out during our intense discussions.

It was about this time that Tina decided that she didn't like Dee. I honestly have no idea why she decided this; who can trace a prepubescent girl's logic? I only know that her decision somehow stirred up the same emotions in me. Suddenly Dee seemed totally unappealing—bland and boring!

We began sitting at a different table during lunch, passing cruel notes, and whispering in the halls. I never talked or even made eye contact with Dee, but Tina began harassing her constantly, calling her names in the halls and talking loudly about her to anyone who would listen. Dee appeared sadder than usual, but kept her air of defiance. Apparently she was just being a good actress, because soon she had Tina and me down in peer mediation with her.

The guidance counselor patiently explained we were there because somebody was spreading rumors about Dee. Tina didn't even bother to hide her smirk, which confirmed what we all knew. I wasn't sure why I had been called down though. When I asked, the counselor reminded me that I had been Dee's best friend only weeks earlier. She forced us to sign a statement that basically said (and I'm paraphrasing here), "We have been bad girls. Let's kiss and make up now; we can still be best friends!"

I didn't think anyone would take it seriously, so I continued with my silence and tried to avoid both Dee and Tina, but Dee called us down twice more within two months, which mortified me. When I asked Tina to stop, she declared me "a whiny bitch" and suddenly the rumors were about me.

Thankfully it was near the end of the school year and I wasn't in any classes with Tina in seventh grade. Dee skipped eighth grade because she couldn't deal with the people from our school and wanted to be up at the high school. I don't blame her at all. In fact, looking back, I should have stopped it.

Through it all, I saw myself as a victim, a martyr, even near the end, but really I was just a coward. If I had said something to Tina at any point, if I had even thought to question her, she would have crumbled. What good is a leader with nobody to follow her? Instead I just pretended that I didn't see what was going on. Most kids had the same attitude, and teachers didn't want to have anything to do with the mess, except for the meddling guidance counselor.

Now that I'm in high school, I see Dee sometimes, walking the halls. She still looks sad, and I still feel guilty, but she's usually with a group of other girls, so it's nice to know that she moved on to better things. It's funny, because I remember thinking that Tina really had it all together, that she had all the answers. In reality she was more insecure than Dee and I put together.

—Anonymous, Pennsylvania

Talking about experiences to others, especially in a group, actually helps girls change their attitudes because a girl who owns her behavior is less likely to engage in the same destructive dynamic again. It is the role of adults to provide girls with the forum to speak about their personal experiences with RA, while making sure adult supervision and input is available.

Stay Connected

Even when it seems your girl doesn't want you to be a part of her life *ever* again it's important to maintain a strong connection with her. Parents—and mothers in particular—are the people girls feel most secure expressing their anger and frustration to after being sucked into an RA behavior dynamic. In the midst of a peer-saturated environment, parents ground a girl and provide a safe haven. While a girl may push away, underneath, she still considers Mom the leading source of comfort and support, as one member of the Warren Ophelia Sister Project describes:

She just tells me to be more confident and try not to worry about what other people think. And that's what I had to do.

When people are calling you names—people who are not including you in their group—or they are spreading rumors about you, it's really hard not to think about that. My mom told me not to let them have that negative impact on me. Sometimes I just had to erase it from my mind and just move on and try to think about the things that are great in my life—I get good grades or I am involved in Ophelia or I am a dance express member or things like that. When something negative happens to me, I try to think of a positive. And what my mom always does when I come home is say, "Honey, this family still loves you. You are still going to go to bed at night and wake up in the morning. You are still going to be able to walk around, have all of your fingers, all your toes," and that just makes me feel so much better when she says that.

If your daughter responds to your attempts to comfort her by slamming her bedroom door in your face, don't give up and don't take her rejection personally. Don't allow her to use the same kinds of aggressive behaviors with you that are troubling her, but keep approaching her, even if you get an angry response. Allow her space, but use notes, letters, cards, and even funny gifts as alternative ways to communicate your caring to her when she seems to reject you. E-mail can be another neutral way to communicate. Sometimes not talking about the RA situation immediately but taking time to go to a movie or watch a show or do something fun together can open the door for a later conversation.

Following is a poem one mother wrote to her daughter to communicate her support and understanding.

> When my feelings are hurt by words that are mean,
> When my heart wants to break and my head wants to scream,
> May I look at the person who's speaking to me
> And think beyond what I initially see
> To what is really going on between us

161

**Girl
Wars**

To what is the truth behind all of the fuss.

*Because what's important is not who is right
Or what has been said in the midst of this fight
But instead what I feel and what I can say
To help both of us find a much more caring way
So I'll turn off my anger and I'll take off the gloves
Turn my words used as weapons into words used as love.*

Celia Straus, author of *Prayers on My Pillow*
      and *The Mother-Daughter Circle*

GIVE HER A TOOL KIT OF OPTIONS

I wish there was a fix-it kit for fights.
—PRETEEN GIRL AFTER A DISAGREEMENT
    WITH FRIENDS

Every girl needs a plan A, B, and C when it comes to making, maintaining, and repairing relationships. Having more skills to draw on in times of trouble will not only make her feel more confident and in control, it will teach her resiliency, a skill that will help her to be flexible and creative throughout her lifetime.

While the wise words of adults might not convince a girl to try a particular approach to resolve RA issues, a suggestion from her peers might. The ideas in this chapter come directly from girls. (To order a framable poster of these tips, titled "What to Do When Words Become a Weapon," see Appendix B.)

Perspective Taking: "I know my family will always love me. That helped me get through all this. When I would come home, my mom would listen, and then she would say, 'Kellie, you know what? We still love you, no matter what.' So I think it helps to remember that no matter how bad a situation gets, your family is still there for you. It puts things in perspective."

Look Beyond the Surface: "I used to think that people who were aggressive really had it all together, but now I know these girls are actually not doing that great at all and they are really having a hard time on the inside. They are insecure and jealous and not very happy. That made it easier for me not to want revenge when they were mean."

Being with Mom: "I don't want my mom to give me advice or try to make the situation all better. I just want her to be there when I need her."

Seeking Refuge: "Find a safe place, a place where you can't be hurt by other girls. This will be different for every girl; it might be someone's house, the mall, church, or wherever. Usually it's someplace where there are rules and someone is in charge, looking out for you. You don't have to worry when you're there. You can relax."

Getting Advice from Neutral Others: "If you have an older sister you can talk to, try it. They've been in the same situation, most likely. I'm lucky to have an older sister. When I talked to her about my friends, she understood instantly. She gave me some ideas on how to change the situation, like being friends with everyone instead of just one or two girls, and not wearing certain kinds of clothes just because my friends were."

Finding Adults You Can Trust: "At school you need a safe, neutral adult. My school nurse is someone I can go to because I know she's not grading me or judging me in any way. I trust her. Teachers usually don't know what's going on."

Mentoring: "Getting involved with older girls really helped me. On my swim team, older girls would say hi to me at school and tell other girls not to pick on me. Any activity where you can find older girls to help you is what I'd suggest."

Making Changes: "Get your schedule changed if it's really bad. Even just changing your lunch period can make a big difference. If your guidance counselor or whoever is in charge won't change it for you, get your mom or dad to call and request it. If you really can't stand it, try to change your whole schedule."

Using Other Outlets to Express Feelings: "Sometimes only my journal is my friend. But if I write about the things that happen with me and my friends, and then look back in the

past and realize, 'Hey, I've gone through this before (and survived!),' it helps me a lot."

Starting Support Groups: "The guidance counselor at my school started a support group for girls. She knew there were a lot of problems, so she created this group for ten of us, and we get together after school and talk, and it really helps. I would suggest asking for a group like this at your school."

Expand Your Circle of Friends: "Don't rely on just one friend. Make lots of friends in lots of different groups. That way if it doesn't work out with one friend, you'll have others to turn to."

Maintain Hope for the Future: "Believe it or not, life changes after middle school. That's the time when problems with friends are at their very worst. There are still things that happen in high school, especially around boys, but I found it so much better."

Keep a Sense of Values: "No matter what happens, don't do anything you don't believe in, like talking about someone else in a mean way. It's not worth sacrificing your beliefs to be popular if it means hurting someone else."

Gain Insight into Why Others Act the Way They Do: "You probably won't think of this at the time, but often the most popular, most relationally aggressive girl has a problem she is struggling with too, which makes her act the way she does. It helped me to think *she* was the one with the problem, not me!"

Act Toward Others the Way You Want Them to Act Toward You: "I found out the hard way: Know who you can trust. Don't gossip!"

Love Yourself for Who You Are: "I think it's really important to accept yourself for who you are. There are some things you just can't change about yourself, and if people don't like you because of them, you probably don't want them for your friends anyway."

"Positive Gossip": "When other girls start to put someone else down, I use positive gossip and find something nice to say

about her, even if it's something really small. I don't let myself get caught up in the bad talk."

Ask Others to Stop: "It bothers me when my friends get caught up in putting other girls down, especially if it's someone I know. When it gets too bad, I ask them to just stop it. Sometimes they listen and sometimes they don't, but at least I tried."

The Little Things: "When I see a girl who is all by herself or who is new at school, I make a point of smiling at her and saying hi even if my friends don't like her. It's a little thing, but I know when I was the new person, it meant a lot to me."

Walk Away: "Sometimes it's just not worth it to stay and be part of a girl trashing you or someone else."

Think About What You Say, and to Whom: "Be careful what you write on the computer!"

Appreciate the Friends You Have: "Let the friends you do have know how much you care about them. Give compliments!"

Popularity Means More in Middle School: "Believe it or not, in middle school being popular seems *so* important, but by the time you get to high school, it doesn't matter as much. Then when you go to college, you realize it doesn't even exist!"

You Are Not Alone: "There are more girls out there who feel like they don't have the right kind of friends or enough friends than there are girls who are satisfied with their friendships."

Help Someone Else: "Doing some kind of volunteer work or community service is a really good way to feel better about yourself. And that's what really matters—helping other people."

Confront Your Aggressor Calmly: "If someone is giving you a hard time, ask her why. What have you done to upset her? Make sure your voice isn't sarcastic or upset when you talk to her. Be sincere."

Speak Up for Yourself: "You have every right to say how

you feel and what you think, as long as you do it in a way that doesn't hurt others. Don't be afraid to make yourself known, but don't be a bully yourself!"

Monitor Your Own Behavior: "It's easy to think that you haven't done anything wrong, but sometimes you have, without even meaning to. Look at how you've acted toward others in the last day."

Be a Leader: "Be the first person in your group to change the things you talk about and do. Invite a new girl to join your group, or change the subject when someone else starts gossiping."

Forgive and Forget: "Sometimes the best thing to do is just move on. Forgive and forget what happened; wake up in the morning and make a new start."

Do What You Love: "Don't let others convince you to do things you don't want to do. Be true to yourself."

Realize That the Way You See Yourself Is Probably Different from the Way You Really Are: "I always thought I was fat, then I saw a picture of myself someone had taken and I realized I wasn't. My friends have had the same kinds of experiences about other things: they think no one likes them, or they're not pretty, that kind of stuff. It's really hard to have a realistic idea of what you're like. When people compliment you, believe them!"

Never Give Up!: "It's kind of stupid, but what Little Orphan Annie said is true: The sun *will* come up tomorrow."

Get a Pet: "My dogs are my best friends. They're always happy to see me, and they never get in a bad mood!"

The following story offers a nice summary of various strategies one girl used to cope with relationship issues.

WAYS TO COPE, KEEPING HOPE

I could talk about experiences where girls spoke hurtful words to me but I mustered the courage to look within myself and ignore them. At times that's just what I did, but sometimes it just wasn't enough.

Once, after a classmate pushed me into the wall at school, her only reply was "Sorry I made you hump the wall!" Granted, she was going through extremely tough times at home, but I wish she'd found another outlet for her anger and grief. I tried to just take a deep breath and let the experience be, which I appeared to do. However, three years later that memory still makes my blood run cold and my stomach tie up in knots. I'm not sure there's anything I really could have done to better the situation. I do know that had I spoken back to this particular girl, I would have only risked more victimization, so I let it be.

One thing I can tell girls who suffer verbal abuse from peers not to do: Don't turn around and take it out on somebody else. I've made that mistake before, and I've regretted it each time. All that ends up happening is I feel bad for making someone else suffer. I, of all people, should know what it feels like to be assaulted with words for no apparent reason. What can you do in the face of a tormentor? Take it out on paper, on the dance floor, on a punching bag. Just don't create another victim.

What's this person babbling about? you're thinking. She's obviously never really been teased the way I have. She doesn't know how much words can hurt. She's never wished she could disappear and never have to face another human being again, for fear of just getting hurt again. That's where you're wrong. You see, I've been through experiences with teachers making hurtful comments and with peers' words being detrimental to any trace of self-esteem that I had left. What helps? It's taken a while to find what does.

I've developed a sense of humor. I'm able to look at those people who criticize me—of which the number has decreased considerably as I've grown up and asserted the fact that I'm here to stay, as I am—and I'm really quite an enjoyable person when people take five minutes to get to know me. I can laugh because these people don't realize how pathetic they are. They could be doing something useful with their time, not just poking fun at me for laughs. Why do they waste so much time on me? They obviously dislike me, so why spend so much time pointing out my faults? I keep telling myself that it's out of insecurity on their parts. Whether or not this is true, it helps.

Another tried-and-true method of nonviolently combating verbal and emotional abuse is finding allies. It helps to know that there are people who know what you're going through. Friends help. Maybe you're painfully shy, and your best friend is your journal. That's okay, it works. You know your journal is a safe place to express yourself. Getting your thoughts out and having people or paper there to support them are wonderful tools in the battle against piercing words.

One thing that I do have on my side is a loving, understanding family. The kids at school (by the way, that's an all-girls school) wouldn't recognize me at home. I can take off my shell, laugh freely, and not worry about judgment. Slowly, though, at school I'm worrying less and less about my classmates' opinions of me. Those who make or have made fun of me—I don't value their opinions. Why should I care what they think? They're clearly not people I enjoy spending time with. I'm happy with the few but valuable friends that I have. They won't laugh at my (correct) pronunciation of the capital of New Hampshire, as a classmate in fourth grade did. They won't yell obscene words at me in the cafeteria just for the purpose of laughing while my face turns red, as happened in seventh grade.

The next time someone chooses to injure you with words, walk away, if possible. Take some deep breaths. Imagine how upset she'll be when you're famous and you make no reference to her in your autobiography.

—Erin Lawton, a teen

Strategies 11 and 12:
CHANGE THE CULTURE
MOTHERS AND OTHERS,
TAKING ACTION

Obviously people who say mothers should just listen
have never had a teenage daughter!
   —MOTHER OF THREE TEENAGERS

The notion that any one person can correct the devastating effects of RA in a girl's life is erroneous. It takes more than mother love to help, or the problem would have gone away long ago! (It also wouldn't be such a challenge for adult women.)

To really begin changing the culture, we need widespread efforts to support girls to spread across the country. The programs described here and in the next section were developed specifically to help girls and the adults who care about them.

GENAustin is a central Texas nonprofit organization that focuses exclusively on strengthening the self-esteem and emotional well-being of adolescent girls. It was started in 1996 by twelve moms whose daughters were in the same Girl Scout troop in Austin, Texas. Having read the book *Reviving Ophelia*, these powerful women, who had been successful in their own careers and personal lives, were amazed to find that there were still serious problems percolating among girls. In their search for solutions, they discovered that nothing was being done to address these issues, so they held a community meeting with a local psychologist as facilitator. When two hundred people showed up, these women knew there was a serious situation that required attention. Their first attempt to address this need was a speakers series on issues related to adolescent girls, professionals, and parents, which was small and neighborhood-oriented.

GENAustin helped spearhead efforts to understand and change RA behaviors in girls. When the *New York Times Magazine* published an article on February 24, 2002, titled "Girls Just Want to Be Mean," a concern arose among local parents. The possibility that some of the material in the article might create competition among girls to hurt others or give girls ideas on how to aggress against others inspired GENAustin to develop a presentation, Girl-to-Girl: Girl Friends, Girl Foes. A regular part of their speakers series, this program addresses the issue of girl-on-girl aggression and provides insight and successful strategies for dealing with ways girls love, hurt, and can heal one another.

The presenters of Girl-to-Girl work with a panel of high school girls to focus positive attention on girl friendships and to remind girls what a good friend acts and sounds like—and what the pain of being victimized feels and sounds like. The program offers some practical advice about how to work out a problem with a friend or, if necessary, how to let that friend go.

The GENAustin speakers series is now the most comprehensive for adolescent girls in the nation, providing more than fifty presentations per school year for workplaces, schools, and communities and usually drawing about two hundred people. Anita Menucci, who was hired as executive director in 1999, estimates that the organization reaches about one thousand people a year, but its goal is to do more. During 2002, the group videotaped three programs that it plans to make available for use by other groups, along with a study guide.

Carolyn Brooks, a middle school guidance counselor and GENAustin board member, has been an active speaker in the series since a friend got her involved two years ago. Her particular interest is girl-on-girl aggression, an interest that began when she did talks on sexual harassment but found that audience questions related more often to girls hurting girls. She explains:

> I keep trying to figure out how to fix it, because I don't believe girls are naturally mean. Sometimes when I talk to parents, they brush it off like that's just the way it is, sort of like saying "boys will be boys." But it doesn't have to be that way.
>
> When I talk to girls, my approach is, what makes them relinquish their power? Why do they give power to another girl? Several girls will come into my office talking about this one powermonger, as I call her, but they can't tell me why this girl has all the power. I ask them why they are giving up these little pieces of themselves and becoming subservient to someone they don't even like. Most times they can't articulate why, but it does get them thinking.
>
> For a lot of girls, being mad isn't acceptable. They don't want to upset others, and they need to learn how to say, "This upset me."

Brooks works on assertiveness with girls, but she cautions that sometimes parents themselves need lessons on relational aggression and healthy communication skills. "Lots of moms of 'Queen Bees' don't seem to realize there is a problem there. It's a bit of denial. They see that their daughter is popular and well liked, and that everyone wants to be with her, but often they don't realize this is because the daughter is wielding power. These moms need to know that their daughters are hurting others. Moms of victims need to be able to listen and acknowledge that this is awful. Girls don't want to hear something like 'It will go away,' or 'Don't worry,' or 'You don't want friends like that anyway,' because it invalidates their pain. Instead, get her to talk, to map out the school, show who goes where—something to get a conversation going to show what it means to her. When a girl can put the experience into words, it becomes less big to her."

Returning to the concept of power, Brooks also encourages mothers to explore with their daughters why they hand over their personal power to another child. She suggests asking, "What is so important about [the aggressor] that you are willing to give up your power to her?"

Brooks credits the success of GENAustin to "women who believe in and are passionate about girls, women who support women, powerful women from all walks of life acting in positive ways to promote the well-being of girls."

Michael Hayes, another regular in GENAustin's speakers series, has worked nationally and internationally in programs for fathers. In addition to having his own teenage daughter, Hayes is a youth minister who currently has a position with a focus on fathers in the office of the Texas attorney general. Ironically, GENAustin approached him when they learned he was offering a series for moms and daughters on healthy sexuality. "They told me, 'We're looking for the best woman to talk on the topic, and we found you!' " He laughs. The four-week session they requested turned into ten weeks, and he has since repeated the series several times over.

His other program, targeted at fathers and daughters, draws crowds of up to one hundred and twenty dads and daughters. Having found that speaking to men only is not as productive as encouraging daughters to bring their dads to programs, Hayes structures short workshops around a concrete activity. His best-received program is a session titled Ten Things Fathers Can Do to Raise Strong, Smart, Savvy, Sassy Daughters. "There's a role for girls to be a little sassy with their dads and get away with it," he explains.

One of the newest GENAustin initiatives is clubGEN, an afterschool program that has mushroomed. The program uses a peer education model of learning, with six to ten high school girls mentoring fifteen middle school girls on a weekly basis. A high school sponsor helps the mentors process the content of their sessions, and an adult from GENAustin is present during the sessions.

During the first year a curriculum was developed to address such topics as self-esteem, relationships (with parents, boyfriends, girlfriends, siblings), and self-confidence, but the mentors are free to explore other issues that are brought up by the girls. Relational aggression is one of the topics that frequently surfaces. Activities accompany the discussions, and both high school and middle school girls emerge from the experience empowered, according to evaluations conducted last year.

"ClubGEN has taught me a lot this year in the fact that I evaluate myself, my friends, and my decisions more closely now . . ." Traci, an eighteen-year-old mentor, says. "I would recommend clubGEN to anyone because I think that it's the best support group outside of your family. It's not biased, it's not therapy or a lecture, just a wonderful diverse group of girls discussing topics that affect them every day." April, age seventeen, declares, "ClubGEN has really changed my outlook in life in several ways. One is that I have become much more aware about myself and safety, and I have also learned how girls think and how to better get along with everyone."

College freshman Miranda Oropeza was part of clubGEN from its inception. "When I was in sixth grade, my family briefly moved away from Texas," she remembers. "When I returned, I thought my friends would welcome me back with open arms, but it wasn't exactly like that. My friend Brittany was friends with another girl, Lauren. I tried to hang out with them, but they turned their noses up at me. Things got so bad that one day Lauren said to Brittany, 'Hey, do you hear something? I think it's the sound of a toilet flushing,' but it was me. Needless to say, I didn't speak to Lauren until freshman year in high school, when she was in my science class and she said, 'I am so sorry I was mean to you. I'm not like that anymore.' It ended up that we had a lot of things in common, and by senior year, when we did GENAustin together, we got to be best friends."

Miranda has a long history of starting her own clubs, including a Big Sis–Little Sis group she formed in high school to be closer to her own younger sister. After pairing up twelve of her friends with twelve of her sister's friends, this talented and insightful young woman had everyone fill out an application describing their interests. She then matched up younger and older girls, who met every month throughout her sophomore and junior years.

Enter clubGEN. "I read an article about GENAustin wanting to start a club," Miranda recalls, "and I thought this would be awesome." She tells the rest of the story this way:

When I called them up, they invited me to their first planning meeting. It was a really cool organization of incredible women from so many different backgrounds; I told myself I'm sticking here, even though I was ten years younger than everybody else. They asked me to present my ideas, so I suggested having teen girls lead the club rather than teachers.

"I went out and recruited girls and got fifteen high school girls and thirty middle school girls who were interested. Then I went to the middle school principal and counselors to set things up with them, and they got me a teacher sponsor. After some training and facilitating of the senior girls we started the actual club. It was awesome. We all formed a close bond with the girls, and it blossomed into a regular curriculum where we would have an introduction, activity, and conclusion every time. We had a stuffed bear that got passed around when it was a girl's turn to speak, and an anonymous box we used so that if we were talking about a topic, everyone would write down their ideas without names and then we took them out of the box and talked about them.

From the very beginning we facilitators were aware there were things we couldn't do and things we might not be able to handle, so we referred the girls on to counselors and teachers or connected them to other resources.

Relational aggression and friendships was the first topic,

which the girls picked up on right away. If we saw that anyone was having a conflict or if there were issues, we wouldn't pinpoint a girl specifically but would talk about the problem in general, and we would try to work that into the next week's topic for the girls. RA was one of the biggest topics; we covered it again and again. The cool thing was that at the beginning of the year not many of the girls knew each other, since they came from all different social groups, but by the end of the year they respected and supported each other. There was even an incident with two girls who weren't particularly friends at the beginning; when some verbal aggression occurred against one in school, the second girl came to her defense. I also got lots of calls from moms saying they had noticed positive changes in their daughters, and not a single complaint. Those things made me feel really good.

Despite her college workload, Miranda remains involved with GENAustin and is helping with a more thorough evaluation of the club. She loves the organization. The girls who were facilitators with her became like sisters to her; she keeps in contact with them even though they are widely dispersed at colleges throughout the country. "GENAustin is a perfect example of women supporting women," she concludes. "It really helped me see how well women can work together."

In addition to the speakers series and clubGEN, GENAustin offers regular activity days, mother-daughter retreats, and an online newsletter that addresses a variety of local and national news. Special workshops for parents and/or girls deal with personal safety, communication strategies, creating positive media, and leadership skills.

A more formal evaluation of both clubGEN and the speakers series is under way, and GENAustin is currently working on packaging the curriculum so other organizations can take advantage of it. Most impressive is the group's commitment to making its programs accessible. "We don't charge fees so we can serve a wide audience," Menucci says, emphasizing that active fund-raising efforts and support from the community make this sharing possible. The group's website, www.genaustin.org, is also a resource for girls and adults, offering an online therapist who answers confidential questions via e-mail, a newsletter, and helpful articles.

A RALLY FOR OPHELIA

*So then all I kept hearing about was Ophelia, Ophelia,
Ophelia. Finally I asked my friends what it was all
about and they got me to join. I only wish I'd done it
long ago!*
— SENIOR GIRL INVOLVED WITH THE OPHELIA
PROJECT

Another grassroots effort dedicated to helping girls also began
with moms. In 1997 Susan Wellman, mother of a teenage
daughter who had struggled during adolescence, read *Reviving Ophelia* and was inspired to find a way to make a difference. She gathered a group of concerned adults to hear author
Mary Pipher speak in Erie, Pennsylvania, in February 1997,
and that was the beginning of the Ophelia Project.

In five short years, the group has evolved into a nationwide
organization with sister project offices in California and
Pennsylvania and new initiatives beginning in Chautauqua
County, New York, in New York City, and in Tampa, Florida.
The project is a nonprofit grassroots volunteer organization
whose mission is to create a safer culture for girls, an effort that
has produced Creating a Safe Social Climate in Our Schools
(CASS), a program that targets all forms of aggression with
a special emphasis on RA. CASS brings together a community of caring adults and high school students to change social

norms by recognizing the hurtful, covert behaviors of peer aggression and identifying a more positive set of normative behaviors. During an intensive two-day workshop, high school mentors are taught to facilitate the intervention program. CASS is currently being implemented in six schools across the nation. For more information on the Ophelia Project's RA programs, go to www.opheliapro-ject.org.

Their How Girls Hurt Each Other program is for middle school communities. As mentors, high school girls tell personal stories about their experience as a girl caught in the middle. Role plays are then created to show different options for the girl bystanders.

"We try to get the girl in the middle or bystander to make a stand," explains one of the high school mentors. "We know that most of the girls we work with have been a bystander at some point. We also know that our greatest chance of making a positive social change really lies with this person in the middle. Most girls are afraid to do or say anything for fear it will come back to hurt them. We try to give them the tools they need to get over the fence and take a stand against RA. Middle school girls are really open to this. They are just scared and don't know how to do this in a healthy way. That's what they look to us for."

Under Charisse's direction, the Ophelia Project has implemented the first longitudinal study of their curriculum to quantitatively evaluate the success of the CASS program. Preliminary results point to the need to change children's normative beliefs about aggression to affect subsequent aggressive behavior. Currently, a more in-depth evaluation is being conducted to examine program effectiveness over time.

Ophelia in Warren

Warren, Pennsylvania, is a small town of approximately nine thousand residents tucked away in northwest Pennsylvania. In March 2002, eight exceptional members of the Warren

Ophelia Sister Project—two impressive women and six self-assured high school girls—traveled from this rural corner of the state to Harrisburg to testify before the Pennsylvania Women's Commission about relational aggression and how the Ophelia Project is making a difference. As the young women role-played a scene involving a victim, an aggressor, and bystanders for the commission, project directors Linda Hackett and Diane Scarcella looked on like proud mothers. They had every right to beam; together these women had launched the first sister chapter of the Ophelia Project and have been busy working with girls ever since.

Diane and Linda are lucky: their tiny rural community has backed their efforts since the beginning, recognizing the need to bolster the self-esteem of girls and foster positive relationships. Says one therapist who was involved early on, "We were concerned about our youth and wanted to translate that concern into action. It wasn't enough to say that we cared; each person in Warren needed to make a concrete investment in our young people. That investment translated into a number of activities that paved the way for an Ophelia sister project."

When Diane Scarcella approached Dr. Hugh Dwyer, assistant superintendent of the Warren School District, for both financial and emotional support within the high school, he readily agreed. "I taught middle school for years," he says. "I know that girls that age need this kind of support."

Diane's reputation as an excellent teacher and community facilitator didn't hurt her case. Speaking glowingly about her other efforts, Dwyer shook his head with a smile. "You just can't turn Diane down." And that is exactly why Linda Hackett found herself drawn in to helping Diane launch the Warren Ophelia Sister Project, even though she too had a full-time job and many family demands. "Diane described this wonderful organization and asked me to become the director," Linda recalls. "When I asked her who else would be working with us, she just smiled and said, 'You and me.'"

Diane and Linda had a surprisingly easy time finding the money in their rural community to pay for the Ophelia Project training program, and a middle school guidance counselor provided referrals of girls who might like to be involved. State Representative Jim Lynch featured the program on his television series in an effort to promote awareness. He believes RA to be "linked with the violence that is happening in the schools. It makes children feel different, 'less than' other children or excluded. Shunning or calling names are aggressive behaviors that often lead to the violence in the schools."

Representative Lynch and his wife, Mary, a member of the Pennsylvania Commission for Women, cosponsored a women's and girls' conference in the spring of 2000. As Mary Lynch recalls, it was extremely successful and helped raise awareness of the Ophelia Project:

> I spoke about the project frequently at commission meetings because a lot of the commissioners are involved with mentoring programs, so there was just a great opportunity to bring it up on different occasions. But it took me two years to get them on the agenda! I know in Ophelia they talk about relational aggression; that's a part of Ophelia but it's not all of Ophelia. I think most people can relate to that more than to some of the other aspects, or they feel that that's an area that can be identified and hopefully reversed.
>
> I think the Ophelia program here is so successful because a rural community works together more as a family unit. I think that Linda and Diane and the energy and time they have put into it are what has made Ophelia what it is.

A senior girl, Amanda, shares her experience:

> I got involved in Ophelia because of one of my friends; it just kept coming up, and there were things in the paper and

it sounded like a really good program. I wanted to be involved, so I signed up for the training.

There were about thirty-two girls and quite a few adults. During breakfast we were told what the *Ophelia* book said and then got introduced to the whole program and what it was about. We broke up into small groups and had discussions about some specific problems that we had at our schools.

One girl was saying how she was a victim and how she was being so verbally harassed and girls were putting signs in her locker and people were trashing her car. It was really bad. I don't see that it's that severe at my school.

Then we talked about how the Ophelia Project tries to help a girl who has relational aggression. About eight of the Warren girls were from the first group to be trained, and they sort of helped the new girls like me and some of the other girls.

We went to the middle school and gave an hour presentation and role play to eighth graders. We had to stop the question and answer session because we were getting so bombarded with questions; once they started, they just kept coming. Some of the girls had written poems for Ophelia and we read them out loud.

For another presentation we role-played and the aggressor wore a specfic color of clothes. We taped cards to her jacket. The cards said different things about what the aggressor looked like on the outside—strong, confident, powerful, snotty, stuff like that. And on the inside, under the jacket, we stuck more cards with descriptions on them, but on the inside they said things like insecure, jealous, and scared. It would make the girls realize that these aggressors aren't really what they seem.

We didn't have teachers in there. The only adult there was the leader. I think the girls were able to open up a little better and talk more because the teachers weren't in the room.

We had some problems with one group of girls, kind of a clique. They said they were always being mean like the aggressor but they didn't think they were aggressors just because they wore trendy clothes and stuff like that. One girl said, "The group I hang out with are always being labeled as mean, and we don't think we do mean things." It was hard to handle, but we just said it doesn't even matter what clothes you wear. If you don't think you are being mean, watch yourself and watch the things that you do. Be conscious and try to do something extra nice for somebody one day, and see if you get any different responses than you normally would.

Then we did the seventh graders. They didn't want to raise their hands to answer questions; we had to egg them on a little bit. But they still did identify the roles correctly. I think they knew what RA was once you explained it to them. They just weren't as responsive.

But when the question and answer session came, we were bombarded with questions like If so-and-so is mean to me, what do I do? It was like Dear Abby. They were about telling us the situations that they have been in and that they didn't really know what to do about. Some of the situations—we were just like "Oh my God." We didn't have any idea what was going on in seventh grade. So that was kind of difficult.

We introduced both of the groups to the Ophelia's Box: this big wooden box with a little split for people to put their questions in. It's in the cafeteria. We said they could write in—they could be anonymous or they could write their name—and we would answer them through the newsletter.

We did presentations at elementary schools too. A few of the guidance counselors came up to the high school one day and said they were having problems at one elementary school and they would really like the Ophelia Project to do a presentation. They were having issues around people who looked different on the outside, people who were of other ethnicities, overweight people who were being made fun of, things like that.

We had to modify the program. We changed "girl in the middle" to "person in the middle" to accommodate both the girls and the guys, and instead of "aggressor" we used the word *bully*. We kept the word *victim*. And we used a brand-new-kid situation.

We passed out stickers to the people who answered questions, but at the end we gave everybody a sticker so we didn't leave anybody out. We did a role play with big signs that said "victim." We thought we would need to have more than one visual aid to keep the attention of younger kids.

Then we broke up into smaller groups, about five kids in each group. We read the book [*The Brand New Kid* by Katie Couric] again, going through it page by page, looking at the pictures and talking about what the words were saying. It's a really, really good book for that level. Actually, one of the boys was a new kid, but he said, "Everybody was nice to me." It was cute. We asked them what happens in the classroom, and they said a lot of things happen behind the teacher's back, when the teacher is writing on the chalkboard or passing out papers.

A lot of the teachers came up to us after the presentation and said it was really good and thanks for coming.

We did start what we call the Ophelia's Advisory Council, open to any Ophelia member. One of the things we are working on is an Ophelia monologue. We want to give a presentation up at the high school to try to make more people aware of what we are doing and get more people involved, people like me a year ago, when I didn't know what the Ophelia Project was. Now that we are doing more and there are articles in the paper and reports on the national news about Ophelia, more people are interested.

I think that you can make a difference with all girls, but the older they are, the harder it is. It is more like a game to them when they are younger; then as they grow older, they just continue to play that mean game. They get into that game cycle of being the mean player of the game and it just keeps getting worse.

Some of the mean girls I noticed in seventh and eighth grades are now involved in the Ophelia Project. They actually got drawn into the program because the guidance counselor got involved and brought them in.

Some of those girls changed, but some who were mean in seventh and eighth grades are mean today. I hear girls going down the hall saying, "She is so mean," or "Oh, she is so rude." It just drives me crazy. I never go down the hall and hear, "Oh, she is so nice," or "Did you hear about the cool volunteer project she did?"

My self-esteem has definitely gone up since I've been involved with Ophelia. I feel that being able to interact with the younger kids makes me more aware of what I do, and I feel better about myself. I'm thinking, Oh, they have started looking up to me and it's cool, and I remember how much I looked up to older girls when I was that age.

The program does create an expectation that you will be different. A lot of times I have caught myself when I was going to say something about so-and-so. And I'm, like, oh, wait a second. A lot of times when my friends start talking in an RA way, I've had to turn the conversation around. We catch ourselves a lot. We are proud of that. We are not proud of the fact that we were going to say something, but we are proud that we thought about it and didn't.

Other strategies used by the Warren group include:

1. Girls are encouraged to buy into the process of changing behavior by being the ones to identify problem areas and intervene. This creates a role for them as part of the solution, not just as part of the problem.

2. As girls mentor other girls, new behaviors are reinforced. Just being a mentor helps internalize anti-RA behaviors.

3. Adult women provide support and encouragement but allow girls to take leadership roles in programs involving girls. (Hence the girls were given the freedom to develop the program for third and fourth graders using Katie Couric's book.) Creative approaches are encouraged.

4. Adults advocate with other key adults in the community, particularly in the schools. In Warren moms made the initial approach to the principal and school administrators to start and support a Cool to Be Kind club.

5. As a group, adults role-model conflict resolution and team-building skills. Girls get to see the power of women supporting women firsthand!

6. Even the high school mentors get mentored by young adult women. Linda's college-age oldest daughter serves as an adviser to the program.

As the first cohort of high school girls involved in the Ophelia Project at Warren prepare to graduate, they agree that their lives have been changed by the organization. This change has manifested itself in different ways for each girl: some have donated their time to raise funds, others have mentored younger girls, and still others have been part of the advisory council. Now, as they go their separate ways to colleges across the country, they will take their Ophelia skills with them, into the next phase of their lives.

CHERYL'S CAMP: IT'S NOT LIKE ANY OTHER

I feel good about myself, and I feel good about the girls around me, 'cause we walk with grace, and we talk with grace, and that makes me feel really good. At Camp Ophelia, we are all united. We are all united.

—GROUP CHANT FROM CAMP OPHELIA

"What can one person do?" a mother asked me recently. "The problem of relational aggression is bigger than any one mom."

Her point was a good one, because the dynamic of girls hurting girls spills over into virtually every aspect of life: school, athletics, church, and community activities. However, not taking action, waiting for girls to "outgrow" distressing situations, or delegating the responsibility for change to teachers or other adults weren't the answers she was looking for.

Before responding to her, I thought back to the summer of 2001, when after finishing my first book about adolescent girls and their moms, I had volunteered to coordinate a camp for young, inner-city girls who weren't old enough to get a paying job or mature enough to be left alone while their parents worked. Knowing that many young women love clothes, I collaborated with a fashion designer friend and came up with the idea of a weeklong camp to produce an outfit designed and created by each camper.

Ten girls showed up the first day, ranging from fifth through seventh graders. They were of all backgrounds, sizes, and colors. Their energy was enormous. Initially it was easy to see the pecking order—who was popular, who was the leader, who were the followers. There was even one little girl who was frequently laughed at by the others, and not in a kind way. Controlling these behaviors was something the program director, who worked with these girls every day, had to devote a lot of time and attention to.

As the week progressed, a remarkable process took place. The girls worked together to draw designs of the outfits they hoped to create and then tore apart old clothes, cut out new ones, and sewed the pieces together, all the while working in teams that changed as their needs did. Gone were the taunts and teasing of the first day, and in their place were girls helping girls manipulate a sewing machine (I was close by!), learn to iron on patches (I was even closer!), and use a needle and thread.

The girls were extremely proud of what they produced, and they complimented one another as well. On the final night of the camp we held a fashion show where each child walked up onstage and modeled the outfit she had made.

Could a group of white, black, and Hispanic girls of these ages have gotten along so well in other circumstances? I don't doubt that they do, because all across the country, young women like these are being guided to use their power in positive ways. At our little camp I had stumbled on just one approach to promote successful interactions for girls, an approach building on teamwork, creativity, and pride in one's abilities. By assigning older girls to help younger ones and encouraging those who were more skilled to share their expertise with the others, the counselors and codirectors were able to foster a sense of group identity that overcame other destructive behaviors.

Remembering that experience, I promised the mother who asked what any one person could do that I would find an answer for her. And I did.

A Week to Remember

It was Friday, June 28. There were twenty girls onstage, their skin color and abilities as diverse as possible, given the small size of the group. While a few of the campers had known one another prior to arriving on the campus of our local community college (one of five generous sponsors who came forward to make the camp a reality), the cohesiveness that had developed among these middle schoolers over the course of five days could not have been predicted.

"At Camp Ophelia . . . we are all united," the girls and their counselors chanted, shaking gourds they had painted earlier in the week. In that moment they *were* united, brought together by a program designed to help them learn about relational aggression, in the form of a camp I had begun to develop nearly a year earlier. As they performed skits and role plays, read poetry, and displayed their artwork for their families and friends in a closing ceremony, I noticed their behavior seemed more genuine than it had on Monday when they arrived. The five young women who worked as counselors had changed too; they were more confident in their ability to influence middle school girls and more aware of how their own behavior could be changed.

Glancing over at Pat and Diane, the two women who had been most intensively involved in the journey to create Camp Ophelia, I felt a surge of gratitude and affection for both of them. We were firsthand proof of what happens when women support and believe in one another, and our relationships role-modeled the safety and security of interactions freed from relational aggression. Even we had learned a better way of "girls helping girls."

Our journey together started in March 2001 at the medical center where I work. I had organized a talk on relational aggression and invited key people from the community, each of whom represented different interests: adolescent medicine, drug and alcohol prevention, counseling and mental health, education, and community service.

It was at that meeting that Pat Gadsden and I first connected. I had heard of Pat through a circle we both traveled in: she and I both volunteered with women at the Dauphin County Prison and their children, but we had never met. On the surface we were as different as two women could be: Pat lives and works in Harrisburg, immersing herself in the culture of youth at risk for substance abuse and other problems through her organization, Life Esteem. A beautiful African American woman with six children, Pat and her husband, who is both a writer and pastor of an inner-city church, are intimately involved in volunteer activities that range from after-school programs in our troubled inner-city schools to abstinence programs for youth aged eight to eighteen.

On the other hand, I live in Hershey, an upper-class suburb of Harrisburg populated primarily by medical center staff and workers at the chocolate factory. There are few minorities in our community, and fewer than 3 percent of the hospital's inpatients are non-Caucasian. Our high school was recently designated a "Blue Ribbon" school, and most of its graduates go on to good colleges without difficulty. (The nationally funded Blue Ribbon Schools Program recognizes schools that are models of excellence and equity, with high academic standards. See http://www.nj.gov/njded/clear/blue.) Despite this privileged setting, I have moved in the same circles as Pat since my family relocated to the Hershey area, first because of my commitment to volunteer work, and later because of my daughter's struggles as an adolescent.

Pat has the warmest smile of anyone I know, and from the moment we began to talk about mutual interests, I knew I had found an ally who had as much energy and commitment to help young girls as I did. Shortly thereafter we were joined by Diane Bates-Sier, a short, funny social worker who added a touch of levity to our intensity. Diane's boss, Scott Spangler, was one of the men at our original meeting in March, and although he remained behind the scenes thereafter, his unconditional support of our cause was crucial over the next year.

Change the Culture

191

Why was Scott so concerned about the welfare of young girls? Not only does he have a daughter in high school, but his previous job was in Warren, Pennsylvania, home of an Ophelia Project chapter.

Fast-forward to the spring of 2002, nearly a year after our first meeting to discuss relational aggression. Pat, Diane, and I have been joined by a number of other inspiring women from various agencies in the Dauphin County area. Our group, the Surviving Ophelia committee, had held another workshop that had drawn seventy-five people from the local area who were interested in the phenomenon of girls hurting girls. Our motivation to continue offering programs was high. Most of our committee members were from community agencies representing diverse interests, and while they were committed to offering time and support, there was no clear strategy for translating that commitment into practice.

Meanwhile I had been busy talking to hundreds of girls and reading every research study I could find on relational aggression. Experts had been approached for interviews, and my briefcase was full of tapes on strategies that have helped girls turn their lives around. Since January 2002 I had been debating the best way to pull these ideas together but still wondering how it could all happen in Harrisburg.

"Camp Ophelia," I finally told Pat over lunch one day. By the time our food arrived, she was sold on the idea and ready to help. We went back to our committee with the idea, and I wrote a small grant proposal seeking funding for the camp, which was rejected.

"We're going to do this," Pat insisted, and then I remembered Scott. Taking a chance, I called him and asked if his agency (Family and Children's Service of Dauphin County) could help.

"What a great idea," Scott responded, suggesting that I send him a proposal. Talking to Diane as well, I sensed that these two were already thinking of sources for the funds needed to hold the camp.

By April I had developed a curriculum, and Scott, Diane, and Pat had located funding. Harrisburg Area Community College volunteered the use of its campus, and other community agencies came forward with offers of (wo)manpower, resources, and publicity. Our committee recruited five senior high school girls as counselors. Although many aspects of the camp were not finalized until early June, we quickly received twenty-four applications from girls in middle school, a group we had specifically targeted.

Any discussion of Camp Ophelia must acknowledge the high level of community support it enjoyed for helping girls learn more positive ways of interacting. Again and again parents and other adults contacted members of our committee about the need for programs such as the one we were offering. Two of our sponsors generously allowed their employees release time to work at the camp, and we received several donations of gifts and food for our campers.

The Friday before camp was to begin, our five teen counselors met with me and two other talented volunteers for a training session. They had been given material on relational aggression to read, so we spent the next four hours on role plays demonstrating the behavior of aggressors, bystanders, and victims; viewing a video on leadership behavior; describing camp activities; and answering questions. Diane, a licensed clinical social worker, and I, a Ph.D. nurse practitioner with a minor in counseling, planned to be at the camp every day and do a thirty-minute debriefing with the teen counselors at the end of each day. For their efforts these young women would be paid $6.75 an hour.

During the week before camp, Pat and I spent every free minute (we are both employed full-time, married, and mothers of teenagers) organizing supplies and snacks, reviewing the activities for each day, and scheduling extra adults to be present at the camp. By Sunday night the first floor of my house had been taken over completely by boxes for each day of Camp Ophelia. My family just rolled their eyes each time I edged my way in the door with more bags of gourds, jars of paint, and rolls of brown paper.

On Monday morning I arrived at the building where camp would be held at seven thirty and found two girls already there. They helped me unload supplies and create signs for directions. Luckily Pat and Diane were there too, and soon we were joined by the other girls and counselors. We created name tags, and personalities began to emerge. We could sense who the leaders might be as the girls went off in groups of four with their counselors to clean gourds as a team. After that we read a poem given to me titled "Nothing Girl," and the campers wrote letters of response to the author.

Then the fun began: each girl lay down on a six-foot piece of brown paper while we traced her outline. With outlines taped to the wall, the process of creating "something girls" took over. Each camper used markers, fabric, beads, flowers, and other craft supplies to individualize her silhouette. Challenged to show us what made each of them a "something girl," they took the task seriously.

Later in the afternoon a friend arrived to drum in time with the girls' gourd shaking, and Pat and I gratefully relinquished the spotlight. A television crew had already shown up to interview me and the girls. Our after-camp meeting with the counselors went longer than thirty minutes because they had plenty of questions and comments. The depth of their wisdom and insight impressed us. By the time everyone left, Diane, Pat, and I sighed in relief. It was 6 P.M. and I had now spent day one of my vacation on my feet for nearly twelve hours!

On Tuesday we continued to work on the something girls and painted the gourds so that they were truly unique to each girl. A second TV crew showed up, and the campers worked on a game called Beauty of a Girl, developed by Pat and Lisa Blanton, one of our volunteers. The game was designed to help girls appreciate inner beauty and to realize how much they shared with one another.

Our campers were incredibly creative and receptive to new

ideas. When I read them stories about relational aggression that girls had shared with me, silence descended on the room; then they quickly came up with role plays about relational aggression they had witnessed or been involved in, and acted them out with their counselors. A second gourd-shaking and drumming activity incorporated the camp chant, written by another committee member/volunteer. By the end of day two, we as staff were in a state of combined excitement over the potential of the camp and anxiety over the limited time available to achieve our ambitious goals.

Wednesday's activities involved the completion of the Beauty of a Girl game, with each camper participating in a "pageant" that celebrated their efforts to create a tribute to the secret partner they'd been assigned earlier. Pat served as a very realistic mistress of ceremonies, finishing by reading a poem about the beauty of a girl, and prizes were awarded for the most creative entries.

With the something girls completed, another activity started: the PowHer Game, which reinforced positive behavior the girls displayed—being kind, helping another, giving a compliment, showing respect, and so on. Girls and staff generated a long list of these behaviors and posted it at the front of the room.

The highlight of Thursday was the creation of "affirmation boxes"—decorated plastic boxes containing upbeat statements created by the girls, counselors, and staff. While it took encouragement to get started, this activity ended up generating a long discussion about positive self-talk when we reconvened as a group. Also on Thursday's agenda was a talk about volunteerism, led by one of our counselors who had gone to Nicaragua for the last three years to build houses with her family. As I heard about the different volunteer activities many of the girls are either already involved in or wanted to learn more about, I marveled that this was a group who had been recently labeled as "mean" by the media. It's hard to believe that girls who seem so earnest in their desire to help others could be inherently cruel to one another.

Friday arrived all too quickly. A newspaper reporter had joined us for two days, interested in the camp because of her concern for her young daughters. Many of the girls shared stories of relational aggression with her and wrote about them for me. Some asked that I read their stories aloud; a few brave campers stood and read for themselves. Well into the problem-solving phase of camp, we again and again pressed the girls for alternatives. How could these incidents have changed? What could they, as individuals, have done to change the dynamics of the real-life situations we had just heard about? Here the counselors had to bring the girls back to reality, gently suggesting that some of their ideas might be easier said than done. It isn't every girl who feels comfortable defending a victim or walking away from gossip, but we came up with multiple strategies to give the girls a Plan A, B, and C. Over and over, the campers role-played solutions until they became comfortable with the new behaviors.

Friday seemed to be the shortest day of camp, although it was full of activity. The PowHer Game was complete: I recognized each girl for her PowHerful behaviors throughout camp, and the girls had their pictures taken with their something girl portraits. Our resident videographer—courtesy of yet another sponsor, the Career Cyber-Café—showed the girls videoclips of their role plays, and everyone rehearsed for the closing ceremony, to be held that night at a local theater, courtesy of Pat's husband. Individual action plans for change during the coming school year were created by each girl, and some were shared with the larger group. Many of the plans were touching in their sincere intent to change the culture of aggression these girls live with every day.

In a personal note to each camper, I reiterated their uniqueness and power, reminding them to "help, don't hurt" others from then on. That night our closing ceremony was a resounding success, with strong family and community support for the girls and counselors, who performed skits about RA and displayed the Blankets of Trust we created, soft squares of material with emblems of friendship glued on.

Although it was only a week, I truly believe our time together *began* to change the lives of adolescent girls. As one of our funders and several of the counselors noted, "There needs to be much more than a one-week camp. This is just a beginning."

With my background in research, I was careful to evaluate every day of camp. As the week progressed, an increasing number of girls were able to understand the concept of relational aggression and identify alternative behaviors. On Monday, the first day of camp, only 26 percent of campers strongly agreed that they knew what relational aggression was; by Friday 83 percent strongly agreed that they knew what it was and knew some alternatives to deal with it.

In addition, 95 percent of the adults who attended the closing ceremony strongly agreed that a program to help middle school girls learn friendship skills was important. Ninety-one percent said they strongly agreed they would like to see more activities like Camp Ophelia in their community.

Relatives of campers expressed their appreciation of the program in their own words as well. Said one stepmother, "I wish the camp was extended. It is important for girls of this age to get to bond and relate to other girls. I'm sure this camp was important to my stepdaughter and helped build her self-esteem." "Thank you for taking the first step in opening the issues to our young girls," another mother said. "These are the issues and concerns that could make or break our girls' path. Having young counselors had a great impact, as they are easier to relate to."

Even the counselors felt changed by the experience and intended to take many of the skills they taught campers back to their own schools. As Leanne, a high school senior, revealed, "I hadn't thought about why some girls do the things they do, like gossip. Now I see it could be related to self-esteem or that they might be jealous. When I went back to school this year, it helped me resolve a fight from the previous year that my girlfriends and I had."

Two mothers of girls who were counselors confided that the

experience was "exactly" what their daughters needed to increase their self-confidence and learn about relationship skills. The father of another commented that it had given his daughter a new perspective on things and had helped her understand how people she had thought were friends took different paths in high school and discontinued their associations. Another father commented that being a counselor had opened his daughter's eyes about some things and awakened a new awareness in her. "It gave her another tool in her relationship toolbox," he observed. "She's learning to use it better and better."

The approach at Camp Ophelia and in our subsequent efforts has been a combination of gentle guidance and arts-based psychoeducational activities. As the arts and medicine liaison at the Penn State Milton Hershey Medical Center and College of Medicine, I appreciate the power of various art forms to open doors to the inner psyche in ways that lectures cannot, especially for teenagers. All the activities of the camp were designed to be both fun and constructive. The program goals were to improve self-esteem, inform girls about relational aggression, have them identify and learn about alternatives to hurtful behavior, and promote in them cooperation, support, and appreciation for one another. Just as we prepare our little ones to begin kindergarten, I hope that someday every middle school girl will be prepared to deal with relational aggression at a time when they are most responsive to changing this behavior. (For information on how you can offer Camp Ophelia in your community, see Appendix B.)

Clearly RA can occur in elementary grades and even pre-school, but it is the girl in early adolescence who has the cognitive abilities to understand and change her beliefs. Seeing this happen during camp, if only on a temporary basis, and working with Pat, Diane, and other adult women dedicated to changing the culture for girls, made my week of vacation more enjoyable and fulfilling (although less relaxing!) than an equal time at the beach. The energy of the girls, as well as their receptivity to learning a better way, gives me a tremendous sense of optimism. *Girls want to be kind to and supportive of one another.* What are we adults doing to help them reach this goal?

DADS AND DEALING WITH RA

I think I have something different to offer, something that helps in a different way.
—FATHER OF TWO TEENAGE GIRLS, DISCUSSING HIS INVOLVEMENT WHEN RA OCCURS IN THEIR LIVES

Too often moms are viewed as the sole healers and fixers of all hurt in a child's life, a belief that causes a mom to feel like a failure when her daughter doesn't have enough friends or the right kind of friends. Unfortunately, the dynamic of RA is so pervasive, the usual comforting and supporting that come intuitively to mothers often need to be supplemented by other efforts.

Joe Kelly, author of the newly released *Dads and Daughters: How to Help Your Daughter When She's Growing Up So Fast* (Broadway Books, 2002), is outspoken about the role of fathers. "The role of dads during adolescence is to stay connected, be aware of and sometimes even counter your first instincts, which are to try to solve your daughter's problems. Being overwhelmingly protective does not help your daughter in the long run." Kelly says that, compared with moms, dads often have more comfort with risk taking, and because they are often working outside the home, they can be a bridge to this world for their daughters. On the downside, dads may have higher expectations for their daughters' achievements.

Kelly recalls an incident when he was really angry at kids who had betrayed his daughters; instinctively, his "papa bear" response surfaced. That was not what his kids were looking for. They wanted comfort and help to process and think the situation through. He believes girls have a very strongly cultivated sense of justice, and in many cases fathers might be more comfortable listening to them ventilate and even encourage it to help them recognize "injustice."

However, not every father is comfortable providing such direction for a daughter. "I certainly think there is a role for fathers," one Ophelia Project dad comments, "but there are certain things I won't want to approach, especially with my daughter. Maybe it's the fear of not guiding her in the right direction; it would be nice if she did come to me on occasion, but there are certain things I think should be handled by the mother. I think dads' discussing daughters with one another is very much limited to certain conversations. We discuss our sons more than our daughters. Occasionally, with a very close personal friend, I'll talk about my daughter, but not to the depth that other friends do who have sons."

If a father only has daughters, he may hesitate to get involved in situations that involve relationship problems. One couple involved with the Warren Ophelia Project discovered they coped differently when an upsetting RA incident occurred with their daughter, the younger of two girls. The mom took action, calling other moms, going to the school, and talking to her daughter. In the meantime the dad encountered some of the fathers of the girls involved in the incident through his work, but his comments were much more casual than those of his wife. "Yeah, I talked to the guys about what happened, but I wasn't nearly as upset as my wife. Maybe that's a good thing, because they got the message that I was concerned and was going to make sure nothing bad happened to my daughter, but I didn't act emotional about it."

Another father reveals that he often tries to help his high school–age daughter deal with RA in indirect ways. "We'll go hunting together," he says. "We spend a lot of time out in the woods and talk about all kinds of things. It's a totally different relationship than the one she has with her mom, but I think it's made us really close."

GENAustin believes the role of fathers is so important, they sponsor a Dads and Daughters Heart-to-Heart speaker on a regular basis. A roster of fathers, including psychologists and community experts, offers programs that address the role of dads during a girl's adolescence. A sampling of their seminar topics suggests key issues every dad should consider.

- A plan to strengthen father-daughter bonds, support daughters in healthy choices, and guide girls toward competence, confidence, and success in career and relationships.

- Steps fathers can take to help their daughters grow in confidence and competence—enabling them to make successful choices both in work and in relationships.

- Ways dads can help their daughters be all they can be. Daughters are encouraged to confide, through a facilitator, those things they need from their fathers to feel more confident, competent, and strong. Dads share with one another what seems to work in forging strong father-daughter bonds. (This program is offered close to Valentine's Day so that dads can spend "a memorable morning with their special 'Valentine.' ")

Dr. Kevin Grigsby, a social worker, therapist, and father of a preadolescent daughter, notes that fathers cannot wait until their daughters reach adolescence to have a relationship with them. The first step is for dads to become aware of their own views and expectations concerning women, because their relationships with their mothers, sisters, and wives will communicate those views strongly to their daughters. Grigsby also encourages dads to talk to one another about their daughters and parenting approaches. In relation to RA, he believes that dads can help girls validate their feelings without minimizing the emotion or leading girls to believe that the behavior is "normal." Sometimes dads are also better able to deal with the extreme emotions that arise with RA.

Carolyn Brooks, the GENAustin board member and guidance counselor, agrees. "I was giving a talk as part of our speakers series, and dads just didn't get RA, whereas moms understood instantly. In fact, two moms who had been extremely traumatized themselves got very emotional about what was going on with their daughters, while the dads needed the dynamics explained to them."

Michael Hayes, also of GENAustin, encourages dads to help daughters cope with girl-to-girl aggression, since the dads can often bring a more neutral, less emotional perspective to the discussion. "The first thing for a dad to remember is to avoid the temptation to rescue or resolve an issue, as we men have a tendency to do. Instead, listen and provide an arena for a girl to discuss her own solutions and any ideas she might have about dealing with the situation. Allow her to test ideas, don't critique them. Next, ask her to identify the reasons why the girl who aggressed against her is important as a friend— what are the things about her your girl values, and what does she wish was different. Ask open-ended questions that give her a voice and help her to explain things.

"Parents aren't very good at open-ended questions— 'What are the reasons this kind of stuff goes on?' 'How can I support you?' 'Do you have any ideas what you would like me to do?'—but they're important. Avoid lecturing. Then just acknowledge that it sucks!" Hayes goes on to say that the single best piece of advice he has for both moms and dads is that when we talk to our kids, our goal should be for the kids to want to talk to us again, not for us to make our point.

According to Hayes, there are other opportunities for dads to connect with their daughters around relational aggression. For example, when he read an article on "mean teens," he shared it with his daughter and asked her how it fit with her experience. "That helped her validate that she was not in it alone, that this was a common experience for adolescents," he says.

A dad can help by asking, "What do I do that makes you feel loved and supported?" since dads have an *idea* of what they do to show love, but this may not be what their daughter *interprets* as love. Lastly, dads need to be patient and persistent; don't expect rewards now, but way down the line. "You'll see results much later," Hayes concludes, "so don't feel it's not working if you don't see a difference right away."

Another expert, Scott Spangler, CEO of Family and Children's Services in Harrisburg and a social worker by background—as well as one of the primary supporters of Camp Ophelia and the father of a Camp Ophelia counselor—encourages dads to try to understand how significant RA is and how very damaging and troubling it can be to a young woman. "You might not see such incidents as significant, but it's important to both accept and validate your daughter's experience. You can do this by taking the time to listen in a nonjudgmental way and even admitting that you may not be familiar with her experience but you want to learn.

"I believe in rational emotive therapy [the school of psychology founded by Albert Ellis], which means you can't change the situation, but you can help your daughter reframe what happened and explore what she's feeling. She can't stop other girls from being mean to her, but she can change her belief system about what happened. Realizing that while other girls may continue the way they are, you can change your response can be very empowering for girls."

Experiences like mentoring can help. After her week as a camp counselor, Spangler's seventeen-year-old daughter Erin gained perspective on both the relationships of middle school girls and her high school peers. "That's the great thing about mentoring," Spangler observes. "It helps both the person doing the mentoring and those they work with."

Like Grigsby, Spangler believes that building a relationship between fathers and daughters needs to start early and takes time. "Closeness doesn't come from 'quality time' you scheduled in for your daughter, it comes from the time you cherish with your daughter. Dads may feel insecure or like they don't know how to relate to their daughters as effectively as moms, but just being there is important. The other thing is to be sensitive to her need to change your relationship with her. You might think there's nothing better than having her sit on your lap, but you need to get beyond that and let her be an adult."

Dave Graybill, father of two teenage girls who also teaches a teen Sunday school class, is bothered by episodes of relational aggression. He recalls a time when "a girl wrote something nasty on my older daughter's car and my hackles went up, but it turned out it wasn't even someone local that they had to deal with regularly in high school."

Graybill works hard to maintain a close relationship with his daughters, who are in high school and college, but says at times it's tough. To stay in touch, he regularly writes letters to the daughter who is still at home, feeling that sometimes they can communicate better that way. He also makes opportunities to be alone with his daughters and goes to Nicaragua every summer with the younger one to build houses for the poor, which has been a bonding experience for them. "If I don't plan these things, the girls would gravitate toward their mom, because she's home all the time. When they were little, my birthday would be the time when I would take them to the mountains, and that would be a big weekend for us. So while I can't say we talk a lot about things like relational aggression, I do get a lot of insight into their lives from these times."

Discussing the importance of extended family, Graybill describes his grandma, who would talk to her grandchildren about not hitting each other when they fought. "She called it 'NBC,' no body contact." Another strategy he uses is to call the parents of his daughters' friends. "I don't hesitate. I'll talk to them about mutual issues and what our children do or say with one another. I get as many different feedback loops from different sources as I can."

Girls concur that they want their dads to be involved in

their lives; girls feel that dads can play an important role by offering a different perspective on situations involving RA. Describing an incident when she had turned to her dad after her friends had hurt her, one senior concluded, "And just him being there—knowing I can count on him is important."

A CLUB OF HER OWN: GROUPS
THAT MAKE A DIFFERENCE

Nobody here cares if I'm not part of the popular crowd.

—MIDDLE SCHOOL GIRL WHO BELONGS
TO A CLUB FOR GIRLS

Young Life is a nondenominational Christian program that is not specifically for girls, but Jolene, a young medical student, shares how her work with this organization touches on issues of relational aggression:

> There was a group of ninth- and tenth-grade girls. We started hanging out with them and talking to them about what they believed in and what they thought about.
> After all of us went to camp, my friend and I left for college. Something happened between two of these girls and all of the mothers were involved too. They weren't talking, and what we did is me and my roommate called and talked to the girls about what was going on, and what was happening. We talked about how you are supposed to love other people, and if you are going to accept this new existing life in Christ, how are you going to act to your friend? So we kind of kept talking to them and I guess it was probably about six weeks or more before they started hanging out again. That was one

incident and it was awful because they got involved in that kind of thing. It just got worse and worse.

We also shared our experiences from high school, and how girls can talk behind each other's back and how it's really important to do what you are feeling in a loving way. We tried to model that with them.

Although not designed specifically to address RA, another organization that regularly deals with relationship issues among girls is the Girl Scouts of America. "If you think about it," says program director Karen Unger, "how girls get along with each other is integral to our program goals, which are to develop self-potential, relate to others, develop values, and contribute to society."

There are many Girl Scouts projects designed to accomplish these objectives, including a new program called PAVE (Project Anti-Violence Education), an antiviolence curriculum underwritten by a federal grant that has already been used to create *En Garde* Against Violence, an antigang fencing program for girls in San Jacinto, and Confidence Counts, a video and interactive website geared toward personal-safety training. The Girl Scout Violence Intervention Project (VIP), for those aged ten to fourteen, provides opportunities to make a difference in one's home community through education and service projects. Especially helpful is an online chart (http://jfg.girlscouts.org/Talk/whoami/Issues/vip.htm) that lists alternatives to violent and aggressive behaviors. For example, one alternative suggests, instead of arguing to make your point, why not join a debating team?

"Since we work with girls from age five on up through teens, relationship skills are woven throughout our programs, just in different ways," Unger says. "A core component of what the Girl Scouts is all about, and which is addressed at every level, is respecting oneself and respecting others. There's nothing we do that isn't teaching girls this important message."

Unlike other organizations, the GSA takes an intentional approach, training leaders and adults to guide girls in relationship skills, requiring an orientation that involves tips on group management and interpersonal skills. The group's online information regarding identifying signs of distress and helping girls cope will benefit any adult working with girls in the middle school age group. A special article on how to handle challenging girls is also available. There are guidelines and books on how to work with groups of girls at each age and a series of activities designed for scouts and leaders to complete together.

The Girl Scout website, http://www.girlscouts.org/index. html, is also packed with information about relationships; there's even an advice column coauthored by "Dr. M.," a psychologist, and her daughter Liz that gives a dual perspective on questions posted by girls. Here's a sample letter and response:

Q: A few months ago I had some really great (or so I thought) friends. Recently one of them met a popular girl and decided to dump me because the other girl hated me. They've turned everyone against me. A lot of people still talk to me, but only for a minute and only until someone better comes along. I know how to make friends, and I'm always friendly in my approach, but it doesn't do any good. Sometimes I feel so depressed that I cry when I come home from school. I have so many secrets I want to share and so many fun times I want to have with one true friend. I don't know what to do! Please answer this because it gets worse every day.   —Cat, 13

A: (Dr. M.) Your letter made it obvious to me that you are a friend worth having. It's too bad that the other girls do not recognize your wonderful qualities. At your age friends often grow apart as interests and needs change. And popularity is seen by many teens as more important than anything else. You might try sharing your feelings (as you expressed them to us) with those friends you really want to get close to again. Perhaps they don't know how deeply their actions have hurt you. If their behavior doesn't change, use the friendship-making skills you know you have to start a new friendship. Lots of girls would appreciate a true friend like you to talk to and have fun with. Be open to finding one or more of them, and reach out to a trusted adult who can help you cope with your feelings of sadness.

A: (Liz) If you can, try to ignore what the girls are doing to you and how they have turned against you. Continue to act friendly and caring. They might realize that you're strong and want to be with you again. But if they can't appreciate you the way you are, you might consider trying to get close to a new group of people who can treat you as a true friend. Good luck!

Membership in the Girl Scouts is ten dollars, a bargain when you consider the safe environment it offers for girls to grow in. GSA resources are available online through the website or via 1-800-478-7248. Although intended for girls and adults who are members, they can be purchased by nonmembers as well.

Built on the concept that girls need to feel safe in their relationships with each other and themselves, ClubOphelia.com: A Safe Place for Girls is a new organization whose goal is to provide safe places online, at camp, in special workshops, and as part of an after-school program. One of the special workshops, e-smART: Safe Places for CyberGirls, explores safe activities for girls on the web and advises girls how to avoid RA interactions. The organization also offers Camp Ophelia, expert consultations on RA, to schools, parents, and organizations. Other features include a newsletter for adults that provides tips from experts and moms on specific relational issues as well as a separate newsletter for girls with the writings of young women about relationship issues with other girls and self-esteem. Quick Cards with strategies for dealing with bullying and other teen issues are provided with each quarterly newsletter, and a PowerPoint presentation, "Sticks and Stones Might Break Your Bones, But Words Can Hurt You Too!" is available. A speakers' bureau, lending library, and workbooks are also available, along with the PowHer Game for Girls, a game for girls to play with peers or adults.

A high school in central Pennsylvania with a diverse student body hosts an after-school program that specifically targets girls in grades eight through ten who are having issues with self-esteem and relational aggression. Each week the Girl Power program meets to conduct activities that promote insight and boost confidence. One of the most successful projects is making a mask of each girl's face, then decorating it inside and outside.

Run by two mental health workers, the club does not involve teachers. Says one of the group facilitators, "I'm not sure what our girls in Girl Power would do if a teacher led the program. I know their feedback about teachers has been varied. A teacher who has good relationships with students may be able to talk with girls about RA or run a group; trust would be one of the biggest factors in their success. By that I mean the students' knowing that their business would not float around the faculty room or with other students. When we talk about teachers with our girls, the biggest complaint from some has been that some teachers gossip about the students. I'm sure this school is no different than others in that way."

The Boys and Girls Clubs of America offer the SMART Girls program, designed to help girls develop healthy attitudes and lifestyles. The program addresses health and social issues specific to female members. SMART Girls is designed for two levels, ages eight to twelve and ages thirteen to seventeen, according to their physiological, mental, and emotional needs. In addition the program is intended to help girls make positive decisions at this critical stage in their development. Specifically, the goals of SMART Girls are to develop and enhance the skills necessary for a healthy lifestyle by helping girls to:

- Understand and appreciate the physical, emotional, and social changes their bodies are experiencing.

- Develop positive lifelong nutritional habits based on the nutritional needs specific to females.

- Adopt healthy exercise routines, including a broad range of physical and leisure-time activities.

- Learn how to access the health-care delivery system in their community.

- Develop and enhance important female relationships through the involvement of adult female role models and mentors (specifically mothers, grandmothers, and other family members).

- Develop communication skills for building cooperative relationships by recognizing and avoiding abusive behavior.

"Living in the twenty-first century, girls today are facing tremendous challenges and pressures," observes Sharon Hemphill, spokesperson for the Boys and Girls Clubs of America.

With all of the choices and decisions young girls must make, preadolescence and adolescence can be confusing and frustrating times in their lives. The rapid growth and physiological changes during adolescence are second only to those in infancy.

During this critical stage of their development, girls feel emerging self-doubts and a growing need for positive reinforcement from their peers. They are searching for independence, but they are still very dependent on support from their families, peer group, and friends. Girls begin to form a consciousness of self to confirm identity and individuality as they experience the transition thrusting them from childhood into puberty and adulthood.

It is important at this stage of a girl's life to offer guidance and help, especially in the areas of social and health-related behaviors. Making a positive transition depends upon several factors: self-esteem and self-confidence; attitudes about their bodies; developing practical life skills; opportunities to contribute to their communities; and the influence of positive female mentors/role models in their lives. As always, it is crucial that sensitive and complex issues be addressed in a safe environment with sensitivity.

It doesn't take a whole Ophelia chapter to accomplish change. Mother, nurse, and wife Debbie Labesky combines her interests in reaching out to girls:

I have seen RA start in preschool and every year the severity of RA increased. Fourth grade in particular was difficult for my oldest child. I joined the Ophelia Project to learn basically how I could help my children, in particular my three daughters, deal with RA. I felt a passion to initiate the first Cool to Be Kind program Cool Club at my children's school. It was based on the Cool Club from the Erie Ophelia Project and has grown to five schools. We started with a half-hour presentation based on a character education topic chosen by school personnel, then I was asked to form the club, which is based on crafts, activities, and community service. But their favorite part is having middle school kids mentor them. Youth respond to youth; they get a clearer message from peers.

I had an eighth-grade young lady tell me in a letter that a few weeks after the CTBK presentation at the elementary school, she had been riding the bus home one afternoon when some RA-type behaviors started. Kids spoke up and said to knock it off—that the aggressor wasn't being "cool to be kind."

Now I have students begging me for the club to meet every week and every month, and have heard from other adults that it is making a difference.

The elementary school principal says about the founding of the CTBK club: "Debbie came to me and then she involved the teachers. First they identified topics they wanted, which gave them some power, and then she developed and presented the programs. The reason it's so successful is that she is extremely popular, extremely enthusiastic, extremely energetic, and, above everything else, extremely caring. Now, I don't just mean for children or adolescents, I mean for humanity in general, because that's the kind of person she is."

DEVELOP YOUR OWN ACTION PLAN TO MAKE A DIFFERENCE

I can't stand by and do nothing.
—MOTHER WHO THINKS HER PRETEEN GIRL
IS A BULLY

A Community of Girls

To build strong, RA-free relationships, girls need to feel a sense of community with one another, even if they aren't "best friends." Team-building cooperative efforts both in and out of school will help accomplish this; just as girls were connected to their grade school classmates in younger years, they can have a larger but still strong community of peers in middle and high schools. Encouraging activities that reflect a constructive joint effort, such as fund-raising, volunteering, or any number of other group projects, will build bonds between girls based on cooperation.

One activity designed for this purpose at Camp Ophelia assigned girls a "secret partner" to observe. Without letting on who their partner was, each girl completed a checklist of information about her and created a collage that reflected her interests. On the day the girls presented and exchanged their collages, campers were amazed to discover how many things they had in common with complete strangers.

Another approach was used by a middle school teacher who held a regular Show and Tell day. The students loved displaying objects that represented important aspects of their lives and discovering interests they shared with one another.

After participating in a skit orchestrated by the Ophelia Project, one eighth-grade girl commented, "This project was the only way I would have ever gotten to know those types of girls. It didn't matter that we belonged to different cliques, we all just wanted to do our best and work together on this. It was fun! By working with them I found out we had some things in common!" Experts in the study of aggression know that sharing collaborative tasks changes the expectations of participants about aggression.

Educate Your Community

Talk about RA to school officials, teachers, guidance counselors, Sunday school teachers, coaches, and anyone who works with girls. After educating yourself, offer to give a twenty-minute talk to interested adults on RA. A good place to start is with any elementary or middle school administrator or groups concerned with parenting an adolescent girl. Most principals are extremely receptive to input, as they recognize the problems that RA poses. One elementary school principal in Pennsylvania observes that RA "starts in second grade, the 'you can't play with me' sort of thing 'because you are not good enough.' It's just like that whole downward trend. It used to be our fourth and third graders and now it's down to second. I see them growing up too fast."

Keep your presentation factual, while covering key points, and use the opportunity to create a group of concerned adults who are ready to develop concerted efforts to change the culture in your community. If you would like help creating an RA presentation for your community or want to order the Power-Point presentation, "Sticks and Stones Might Break Your Bones, but Words Can Hurt You Too!," see Appendix B.

Keep Learning

Start a book club or issues group to encourage adults to learn more about RA and take action to alleviate it. Local libraries, often a place where girls congregate, are always interested in new programs. Offer to coordinate a group that will discuss books devoted to RA. For your convenience, a reference list can be found in Appendix A.

Key Points

Now that you understand the dynamics of RA and have your own set of strategies to help combat female bullying, you can take action in your own home and community. As you put together a plan and educate others about RA, keep these talking points in mind:

* Girls are not inherently mean! This book is about empowering girls to make better choices and creating an environment that can guide girls toward constructive rather than destructive choices. Together, we advocate creating a new culture that will bring out the best in girls.

* Power and RA go hand in hand. Girls are no different from the rest of society when it comes to the need to be close and connected to others. However, we live in a culture that teaches independence, competition, and achievement at all costs. How we choose to connect is reflected in our social interactions with one another. The key to our approach is teaching girls how to connect in emotionally safe ways; we encourage girls to connect without being motivated by power.

* Peer relationships need to be balanced by adult relationships. Parents (both mom and dad) need to stay connected to their adolescent girl, even when she doesn't seem to want that.

* Girls need to learn multiple alternatives to aggressive behavior. There is no "right" answer here. The key is to provide

unconditional support for our girls against the backdrop of healthy accountability.

- Activities and messages need to be fun, creative, and stimulating for girls. Use cooperative, meaningful tasks to create a sense of belonging.

- Trust is the cornerstone of all healthy relationships. Look for ways to build trust among girls, as well as between caring adults and girls.

- Be sensitive to developmental issues. Adolescent girls are experiencing dramatic physical changes (the typical weight gain during puberty is thirty-eight pounds!), changes in how they think, and changes in the way they feel about themselves—all while still trying to maintain healthy connections with their parents. Add to this their increasing need for intimacy and you have an exciting and challenging time!

- Change beliefs about RA. Both adults and girls need to understand that RA is not "normal," that it exists on a continuum of mild to severe, that it is caused and perpetuated by insecurity on the part of victims, bystanders, and aggressors, and that the damage can be long-lasting.

- Extend your girl's support network. A support network is essential for your girl. Whether it consists of extended family or other adults doesn't seem to matter, as long as she can rely on a network of people who care about her.

- Remember the principle of confident kindness. Girls who feel good about themselves can be kind to others without being taken advantage of or manipulating.

You're set! If you need a structured next step, use the following to guide you on.

Step One: Become a champion or find one in your community. As you could see again and again in this book, change occurred because one or two people felt strongly about issues connected to relational aggression. That's all it takes to get started!

Perhaps you aren't the most outgoing or confident person but still want to begin a grassroots effort in the community where you live. Gather the information you need to talk knowledgeably about changing the culture of female aggression. If your audience needs to be educated, refer back to the beginning of the book; if they're already savvy, consider the talking points above. Distribute the information to schools, doctors' offices, and churches. If you shy away from public speaking, find a friend who will volunteer to give free talks. Women's groups, community organizations, school meetings, and libraries are all ideal venues for presenting these seminars where you will be able to enlist the support and help of others.

Identify influential people in your community and persuade them to become champions. What makes a champion? Passion of the kind displayed by Sue Wellman, founder of the Ophelia Project, or GENAustin's initial members. Look for individuals who are willing to work hard to create a new culture. If you can't think of any influential people you would be comfortable approaching, combine forces with other adults concerned about preteen and teenage girls.

Don't forget to include girls at this point, and in every subsequent step. Listen to what they have to say; they are your true experts. Involving a diverse group of girls and empowering them with a key role in your program will enhance ownership and buy-in, essential parts of any program.

Step Two: Form a group. You may be a stay-at-home mom who has access to other moms who can meet during the day, or you may be a dad who can mobilize a group of fathers for a "dads and daughters" breakfast that can launch other efforts. Perhaps your faith community might become involved in conflict resolution, or other women at your workplace may meet with you over lunch to discuss common concerns. A tried-and-true approach is to have a book discussion group or to bring in a speaker to talk to your community about relational aggression. (That's how GENAustin and the Ophelia Project both got launched.) It only takes one meeting to get started!

Step Three: Identify a single, highly visible but solvable problem. You might decide to address the issue of girls hurting girls on sports teams or institute a day of caring that involves volunteer work. Whatever the issue you decide to tackle first, make it one that will get you lots of attention and further volunteer interest. Creating a forum for girls to present their developmental issues and garner support can be a powerful way to discover issues and direct your efforts. It's always a good idea to include someone with a clinical background (social worker, guidance counselor, etc.) in these efforts, should participants need additional follow-up.

Step Four: Hold a workshop to discuss a strategy for solving that one problem. This may involve any of the specific strategies discussed in this book—a camp, a girls' group, a mentoring program, or even just a larger workshop to build a coalition in your community. Your approach should be comprehensive, meaning that the earlier (younger) you can get to girls, the more likely you are to change the situation for the long term. Matching up "big sisters" in middle school with "little sisters" in elementary school and charging them with being a support system during the early weeks of school is one example, suggested by a senior girl, of how girls can be encouraged to help rather than hurt one another.

Step Five: Begin the intervention with the help of the key players from Step Four and the group you formed in Step Two. Remember to keep girls actively involved! High school and early-college-age girls in particular may be a creative and inexpensive resource for you, and mentoring has been shown to provide a vehicle for positive lasting change. To change the way girls connect with one another, activities and messages need to include mentoring, whether high school students are paired with middle school students or college students with high school students or adults with college students. Some schools will even offer students academic credit for providing community service such as the kind you seek.

As you plan your program, make it activity-based, with cooperative learning tasks that require everyone to participate. Set up clear behavior guidelines ahead of time and clearly communicate the rules. If you have access to someone who can incorporate art and creativity in your activities, girls will view participation as fun and recreational as opposed to just more school.

Step Six: Implement the program. Make sure to role-model well!

Step Seven: Evaluate whether the goal you established in Step Three was achieved. The evaluation doesn't need to be fancy, elaborate, or formal. Interviews with those who were involved are the easiest, quickest way; we can provide some questions to ask. If you need more sophisticated evaluation for funding purposes, we can help with that too.

Step Eight: By now, the community will have begun to address RA. Other problems that need to be addressed will surface. Start back at Step Four and repeat!

Step Nine: Consider making your group an ongoing organization, electing officers, etc. Fund-raising is also helpful. Again, there are people in your community who know how to do this, or we can help.

Step Ten: Once you have credibility, you are the champion who can pull together community agencies, schools, moms' groups, dads' groups, places of worship, etc. You're on your way!

Final Message

It is our hope that every girl who reads this book, as well as every girl whose life is touched by an adult who reads this book, will echo the sentiments of a simple poem penned by

Erika Taylor, a twelve-year-old participant in Camp Ophelia who shared her thoughts during our final reception.

I Can

I can overcome my fears
I can buy for the hungry
I can help stop pollution
I can give advice
I can receive
I can listen
I can think
I can teach
I can know
I can give
I can feel
I can see
I can.

APPENDIX A
WEBSITES AND OTHER RESOURCES

WEBSITES

These sites contain a mix of adult and adolescent information. It's always a good idea to check out any URL before sending your girl there.

http://www.academic.org/

Expect the Best from a Girl is a wonderful site from the Women's College Coalition. In addition to tips for parents and a section on female role models, a special plus is A Sampling of Programs for Girls (http://www.academic.org/programs.html), which describes programs all across the country designed to help young women make smart, successful choices for their lives.

http://atdpweb.soe.berkeley.edu/quest/home.html

Just for girls to learn about themselves, career options, and positive female role models.

http://www.beinggirl.com/

Created for teens by the makers of Tampax, this site has a variety of resources, including explicit content on reproduction. Fun activities include Self-Discovery, Laugh Out Loud, and Your Turn. Girl Vine features Cool Customs: Dating and Marriage Around the World.

http://www.bygpub.com/books/tg2rw/volunteer.htm

20 Ways for Teenagers to Help Other People by Volunteering is part of the website for *The Teenager's Guide to the Real World,*

a book by Marshall Brain. Descriptions of volunteer programs and links to other resources are available.

http://www.educatingjane.com/

Get updated, get involved, and learn a lot in the process with the help of Educating Jane!

http://education.indiana.edu/cas/adol/adol.html

An electronic guide to information on adolescent issues from the Center for Adolescent Studies at Indiana University. Helpful information for both adults and girls.

http://femina.cybergrrl.com/

One of the few (if not the only) site search engines just for girls!

http://www.fullcirc.com/teens.htm

Full Circle Associates provides a listing of interactive teen sites related to such issues as activism, mentoring, violence, health, advocacy, and the media and communications.

http://www.girlsplace.com/

A site that offers girls tips on self-esteem, coping, and balance.

http://www.girlpower.com/

This site, developed by author Hillary Carlip, encourages positive womanhood and self-esteem by publishing powerful stories written by teen girls.

http://www.girlpower.gov/

From the U.S. Department of Health and Human Services, this site has separate sections for grown-ups and girls, as well as research and news about girls.

http://www.iemily.com/

Website dedicated to promoting health and awareness in teen (girl) lives.

http://www.independentmeans.com/

Helps girls to become financially independent by offering suggestions, guidance, and counseling.

http://www.self-esteem-nase.org/

Website for the National Association for Self-Esteem. Helpful information for adults and teens with a line of products that help explore and promote self-esteem. Given a five-star rating by the Child & Family WebGuide.

http://www.smartgirl.com/

Reviews and details on everything from websites to body-care products, magazines, and television shows. Opportunities to Speak Out, Express Yourself, and Spread the Word. Developed by the National Science Foundation and the University of Michigan.

http://www.teenadvice.org/

You ask a question; they are there to help!

http://www.teenalways.com/teen/older/pages/y_home.jhtml

This site is sure to answer whatever nagging "female question" you've always wondered about.

http://www.teenwhispers.com/

Share your thoughts, ideas, and problems with those who can help.

http://www.terrifichick.com/index.html

Learn to be yourself through articles, columns, and resources.

MOVIES

The following movies were selected not for their artistic merit but for their relevance to the topics discussed in this book. They provide an excellent opportunity to stimulate discussion between adults and adolescents on a variety of issues. Please check the movie's description and rating before deciding to view it with girls of different ages.

Anywhere but Here (1999)

Based on a wonderful book by Mona Simpson, this story about a mismatched single mom and her teenage daughter captures many adolescent issues related to self-discovery and relationships.

Bring It On (2000)

The poised and happy captain of an affluent cheerleading team discovers that one of her teammates has stolen routines from an impoverished urban team. Both teams will compete for a national title.

Clueless (1995)

A young woman compensates for her own loneliness and insecurity by being a social do-gooder, along with her best friend. Together they "make over" a new girl who comes to their school.

Emma (1996)

A lighthearted adaptation of Jane Austen's novel examines the busy life of a young woman engaged in gentle gossip and energetic matchmaking on behalf of a girlfriend.

Ever After—A Cinderella Story (1998)

A reinterpretation of the old fairy tale, in which an empowered heroine takes matters into her own hands and uses her brains and beauty to overcome unfortunate circumstances.

Heathers (1989)

Although this movie has dark undertones, it captures all the dynamics of RA between two girls through the story of Veronica, who is part of a clique called Heathers and sometimes wishes her friends were dead.

A League of Their Own (1992)

Comedy about a struggling team in the All-American Girls Professional Baseball League, formed when there weren't enough men's baseball teams during World War II.

Little Women (1994)

Check out this adaptation of Louisa May Alcott's novel, which describes the life of four sisters growing up in New England during the Civil War.

Mermaids (1990)

This coming-of-age story features two sisters and their flamboyant single mom, played by Cher, who move into a small Massachusetts town in the early '60s.

Mystic Pizza (1988)

A comedy about the ties among three blue-collar sisters who work in a pizzeria in tiny Mystic, Connecticut. A good example of girls supporting girls.

National Velvet (1945)

The classic family film starring a spunky twelve-year-old Elizabeth Taylor, who ends up riding her horse in the Grand National Steeplechase.

Never Been Kissed (1999)

A newspaper journalist who was unpopular in high school is assigned to return and write an undercover story about teens. As she relives her experience, viewers gain perspective on the superficiality of popularity and the long-term importance of brains and integrity.

Pretty in Pink (1986)

When a girl from a poor family connects with a boy who is wealthy, she has to examine what kind of person she is really is and wants to be. Also shows the value and hurt that can come from friends.

She's All That (1999)

An unpopular girl gets invited to the prom by a popular guy who takes her out as part of a bet with his buddies. He learns that his actions have far-reaching consequences, and she learns to deal gracefully and confidently with the cruelty of peers.

So Little Time: Vol. 1 (School's Cool) (2001)
and *Vol. 2 (Boy Crazy)* (2001)

Based on the television series starring teenage twins Mary-Kate and Ashley Olsen, who can at times seem a bit stereotyped but who deal with a variety of important relationship issues.

Some Kind of Wonderful (1987)

This movie contrasts the personalities of two girls who are both involved, in different ways, with the same boy; it explores issues of integrity and values. There's even a tough-guy bully to deal with.

Steel Magnolias (1989)

Although this movie is about adult women, it illustrates the value of women supporting women and the enduring bond between mothers and daughters.

10 Things I Hate About You (1999)

A popular and pretty girl is faced with a dilemma: her dad won't let her go out with a boy she likes until her unpopular, rebellious, boy-hating older sister Kat gets a date of her own.

BOOKS

Some of these books are geared primarily for girls, others for adults. Adults can often learn as much from material intended for adolescent audiences as from more mature content.

Brave New Girls: Creative Ideas to Help Girls Be Confident, Healthy & Happy

By Jeanette Gadeberg and Beth Hatlen (illustrator) (Fairview Press, 1997)

This hands-on book is a great resource for both adults and girls, offering creative activities that will help teens develop self-confidence and self-esteem.

Cool Women

By Dawn Chipman, Mari Florence, Naomi Wax, Lisa Ling, and Pam Nelson, eds. (17th Street Press, 2001)

An inspiring book that offers female role models from around the world and across generations.

Every Girl Tells a Story: A Celebration of Girls Speaking Their Minds

By Carolyn Jones (Simon & Schuster, 2002)

A photo-essay book by a noted photographer and the Girl Scouts of America, featuring more than eighty girls who share stories of their lives and ambitions.

Finding Our Way: The Teen Girls' Survival Guide

By Allison Abner, Linda Villarosa (contributor) (Harper-Perennial, 1996)

Written by two African Americans, this guide for girls in grades eight through twelve deals with many topics relevant to teens, addressing multicultural differences in issues such as body type.

Getting It Right with Teens

By Madeline Swift (Childright, 2000)

Advice on how to maintain the close relationships you enjoyed during childhood with your teen, and to reinforce her value of respect, self-discipline, accountability, and integrity.

Girl in the Mirror: Mothers and Daughters in the Years of Adolescence

By Nancy Snyderman and Peg Streep (Hyperion, 2002)

Moms who inform themselves about the challenges of adolescence are better able to help their daughters, especially since these struggles often occur when mothers are going through their own major life changes.

The Girls' Book of Wisdom: Empowering, Inspirational Quotes from Over 400 Fabulous Females

By Catherine Dee (Little, Brown, 1999)

Advice from well-known women including Gwyneth Paltrow, Maya Angelou, Lauryn Hill, Whoopi Goldberg, Eleanor Roosevelt, and many others on a variety of topics relevant to adolescence.

Websites and Other Resources

The Girls' Guide to Life: How to Take Charge of the Issues That Affect You

By Catherine Dee (Little, Brown, 1997)

This book provides girls aged ten to fifteen with advice, reassurance, and empowerment.

Girls Seen and Heard: 52 Life Lessons for Our Daughters

By the Ms. Foundation for Women, Sondra Forsyth, and Carol Gilligan (preface) (Putnam, 1998)

An attempt to counteract the messages girls are given by society using collaborative assignments between adult and young women. Uses fifty-two "life lessons" to help explore ways to appreciate and develop character and strength.

Girls to Women: Women to Girls

By Bunny McCune et al. (Celestial Arts, 1998)

Writings from around the world by young and adult women as well as fathers, designed to help provide insight and support during transition from girlhood to womanhood.

Girltalk: All the Stuff Your Sister Never Told You

By Carol Weston (HarperPerennial, 1997)

The third edition of a collection of information and letters from teens that offers a guide to nearly every problem a girl from eight to eighteen might face.

Girl Wars: 12 Strategies That Will End Female Bullying

By Cheryl Dellasega, Ph.D., and Charisse Nixon, Ph.D. (Fireside, 2003)

A solutions-based book on relational aggression that offers both adult and adolescent readers of all ages the opportunity to learn how to combat relational aggression (RA).

Girl Wise: How to Be Confident, Capable, Cool, and in Control

By Julia Devillers (Prima Publishing, 2002)

More than one hundred experts tell you how to deal with big and little challenges teen girls face on the journey to confident womanhood.

Odd Girl Out: The Hidden Culture of Aggression in Girls

By Rachel Simmons (Harcourt, 2002)

An in-depth exploration of relational aggression that names and describes this phenomenon using the real-life stories of girls.

Ophelia Speaks: Adolescent Girls Write About Their Search for Self

By Sara Schandler (HarperPerennial, 1999)

A compilation of stories by teenage girls, written to respond to the bestselling *Reviving Ophelia* (see below). In the words of girls who are dealing with suicide, depression, cutting, eating disorders, popularity, and numerous other issues, this book offers insight and affirmation for adults and adolescents alike.

Picture the Girl: Young Women Speak Their Minds

By Audrey Shehyn (Hyperion, 2000)

Another book of photo-essays on thirty-five teenage girls from diverse backgrounds who speak about their concerns and strengths.

Protect This Girl: Words of Inspiration from Girl to Girl

By Zoe Stern (Tricycle Press, 1999)

A book of art and quotes for adult and young women, with tear-out pages that can be posted or mailed to others.

Queen Bees and Wannabes: Helping Your Daughter Survive Cliques, Gossip, Boyfriends, and Other Realities of Adolescence

By Rosalind Wiseman (Crown, 2002)

Descriptions and advice for moms of teenage girls related to specific challenges during the adolescent years. If you need help figuring out whether your daughter is keeping secrets or deceiving you, or if you need to figure out how to deal with your own emotions, here's a book full of information.

Raising Strong Daughters

By Jeanette Gadeberg (Fairview Press, 1996)

Written by a clinical social worker and founder of Raising

Strong Daughters, Inc., this book advises parents on how to raise a girl who is self-confident and successful.

Reviving Ophelia: Saving the Selves of Adolescent Girls
By Mary Pipher (Ballantine Books, 1992)

A classic about the enormous negative pressures placed on teenage girls by society. Written by a psychologist who found many of her female clients were struggling to survive the teenage years and developing such serious problems as eating disorders and depression as a consequence.

Surviving Ophelia: Mothers Share Their Wisdom of the Tumultuous Teenage Years
By Cheryl Dellasega (Ballantine Books, 2002)

Stories from mothers of teenage girls offer readers advice on how to deal with issues such as eating disorders, substance abuse, and other developmental challenges.

Things Will Be Different for My Daughter: A Practical Guide to Building Her Self-Esteem and Self-Reliance
By Mindy Bingham, Sandy Stryker, Susan Allstetter Neufeldt (contributor) (Penguin USA, 1995)

An interactive book featuring checklists and questions to help parents explore their own feelings, by authors with a track record of publications for girls on career choices, self-awareness, and other issues.

33 Things Every Girl Should Know: Stories, Songs, Poems, and Smart Talk by 33 Extraordinary Women
By Tonya Bolden (Crown, 1998)

This is a book to build girls up, using advice from noted adult women who share their work to provide adolescent girls with insight and support.

200 Ways to Raise a Girl's Self-Esteem: An Indispensable Guide for Parents, Teachers, and Other Concerned Caregivers
By Will Glennon (Conari Press, 1999)

A checklist of behaviors for parents and others to use in helping daughters negotiate the complex world of adolescence, when girls often get negative societal messages about athletics and intelligence, among other things.

Woman's Inhumanity to Woman
By Phyllis Chesler (Thunder's Mouth Press/Nation Books, 2002)
Written by a hard-core feminist, this lengthy book describes how adult women often betray, hurt, and humiliate one another.

The Wonder of Girls: Understanding the Hidden Nature of Our Daughters
By Michael Gurian (Pocket Star, 2002)
This discussion of how girls grow and develop, presented by a therapist, also covers special topics that confront adolescents. Some readers may be offended by the author's views, which are antifeminist.

APPENDIX B
RESOURCES AVAILABLE
THROUGH CLUBOPHELIA.COM

Consultation Services

A team of expert consultants available for group or individual consultation, public speaking, or workshops

Curriculum Guides for Club Ophelia, Camp Ophelia, and e-smART: Safe Places for Cyber-Girls

PowerPoint presentation: "Sticks and Stones Might Break Your Bones, but Words Can Hurt You Too!"

A twenty-minute slide presentation on RA with handout, designed for public education

The PowHer Game for Girls

Board game on powerful behaviors that uses situations for girls to resolve RA dilemmas

"Relational What?"

Professionally designed two-page flyer on RA facts; mass quantities available

Wary Mary or Savvy Sue: Which Are You? A Primer of RA Facts for Girls

Professionally produced booklet with illustrations containing girls' stories about RA and discussion guide

"What to Do When Words Become a Weapon"

3' x 5' professionally produced poster containing tips from real girls on how to deal with RA

WHAT'S YOUR RA QUOTIENT?

Think about your behavior in the last week. Check off each time you have done the following:

1. _____ Called other kids names that make fun of them?

2. _____ Said something about someone else that you knew wasn't nice?

3. _____ Walked away when your friends started talking about someone else you know?

4. _____ Laughed when someone else made fun of another girl?

5. _____ Written a note or graffiti about someone else that wasn't nice?

6. _____ Felt put down by someone but not spoken up about it?

7. _____ Asked your friends to stop talking about another friend who wasn't there?

8. _____ Let someone else talk you into doing something you didn't really want to do?

9. _____ Refused to talk to someone so it would upset her?

10. _____ Invited a new girl to sit with your crowd at lunch?

11. _____ Repeated a rumor you heard about your friend?

12. _____ Started a rumor about a girl who was mean to someone else?

13. _____ Made fun of another girl's clothes, hair, or appearance?

14. _____ Stood up for another girl your friends were making fun of?

15. _____ Sent an e-mail to someone that said something negative you wouldn't say in person?

16. _____ Been the target of a rumor?

17. _____ Threatened someone because she made you mad?

18. ____ Gone to sit with someone who was by herself and sad?

19. ____ Listened to gossip about another girl?

20. ____ Received messages in a chat room that hurt your feelings?

21. ____ Tried to sit with a group of girls at lunch and been told you couldn't?

22. ____ Excluded someone to make her feel bad?

23. ____ Cried or felt sad because of something mean another girl did to you?

24. ____ Helped another girl with her homework, even though your friends say she is stupid and will never be able to understand the assignment?

25. ____ Made a new friend?

26. ____ Been part of a crowd of girls who watched as your leader made fun of another girl?

27. ____ Deliberately done something you knew would hurt someone?

What's Your RA Quotient?

28. _____ Took something that belonged to someone else just to bother her?

29. _____ Wanted to speak up and defend another girl, but didn't because you were afraid?

30. _____ Had to sit by yourself in class because your friends decided to move away from you?

31. _____ Complimented a girl you don't know very well on her outfit?

32. _____ Tried to convince others to be mean to someone or to ignore her?

33. _____ Done something to embarrass a girl you don't like?

34. _____ Threatened not to be friends with someone if she didn't do what you wanted her to?

35. _____ Stayed and watched one girl be mean to another?

36. _____ Dared someone to do something she didn't want to?

37. _____ Insulted someone verbally because she looked at you the wrong way?

38. _____ Wrote something unkind about a girl you don't like in a public place, without signing your name?

39. _____ Called a girl you don't like an unkind name when she could hear you?

40. _____ Listened in when a friend called another girl and tried to get her to talk to you?

41. _____ Made up something to get a former friend in trouble?

42. _____ Given a friend a compliment?

43. _____ Teased a girl you know but not very well?

44. _____ Deliberately ignored a girl you don't like when she said hi to you?

45. _____ Stayed friends with someone because you were afraid of what she would do if you didn't?

46. _____ Been teased by someone else about the way you look?

47. _____ Excluded someone from your group because your friends told you to?

48. _____ Looked or gestured at someone in a way meant to hurt or insult her?

49. _____ Been in a chat room but not participated when a girl you know got flamed by your friends?

50. _____ Forgiven a friend who hurt your feelings?

Chances are you've used some if not all of these behaviors in the past week. Check and see which of the following you used the most.

Aggressive Behaviors:
1, 2, 5, 9, 11, 12, 13, 15, 17, 22, 27, 28, 32, 33, 34, 36, 37, 38, 39, 41, 43, 44, 48

Bystander Behaviors That Support Aggression:
4, 19, 26, 29, 35, 40, 47, 49

Behaviors Checked Off by a Victim:
6, 8, 16, 20, 21, 23, 30, 45, 46

Power Behaviors; Congratulations!:
3, 7, 10, 14, 18, 24, 25, 31, 42, 50

APPENDIX D
CONFLICT RESOLUTION SKILLS

The following are selected skills that promote a peaceful resolution of conflict and disagreement. They were adopted from the Conflict Resolution Network, www.crnhq.org.

1. Adopt a win/win approach that respects all parties' needs.

2. Turn problems into opportunities for creative solutions and relationship building.

3. Use empathy to listen, clarify, and signal understanding.

4. Be assertive: discuss the problem, not the person.

5. Express emotions appropriately.

6. Be willing to work on the issue until it is resolved.

7. Identify your issues and allow others to do the same.

8. Brainstorm options; list as many as possible.

9. Try to see the problem from other perspectives.

About the Authors

Cheryl Dellasega, CRNP, Ph.D., author of the bestselling *Surviving Ophelia: Mothers Share Their Wisdom in Navigating the Tumultuous Teenage Years*, has developed and presented numerous programs for mothers and daughters, including Camp Ophelia, a one-week camp created especially for middle school girls that uses creative arts, mentoring, trust building, connectiveness, volunteerism, and activities to enhance self-esteem and effectively deal with relational aggression, and Club Ophelia, an after-school program that continues the work begun in camp. Currently, Dr. Dellasega leads a group of community representatives that is targeting relational aggression in schools and organizations in Harrisburg, Pennsylvania. Cheryl lives in Hershey, is married, and the mother of three children, including a teenage daughter. She is on the faculty of the Penn State College of Medicine in Hershey, Pennsylvania, where she leads workshops on arts and healing, teaches medical students, and conducts research on health-related topics.

Charisse L. Nixon, Ph.D., relational aggression researcher and Ophelia Project board member, has used her academic expertise and research skills to help create stronger programs on relational aggression such as *High Aspirations*, a training program that educates teachers on the factors that affect girls' academic achievement, and a comprehensive adolescent mentoring program serving both inner city junior high and suburban high school students. Dr. Nixon teaches a variety of courses in the Department of Psychology at Penn State Erie, with her current research focusing on the overriding implications of prevention and intervention efforts in the field of relational aggression. She spends a large portion of her time traveling to speak to teachers, administrators, parents, and adolescents about relational aggression. She lives in Erie, Pennsylvania, with her husband and two young daughters.